THE EAST END IN COLOUR 1980-1990

THE EAST END IN COLOUR 1980–1990

TIM BROWN

edited by

Chris Dorley-Brown

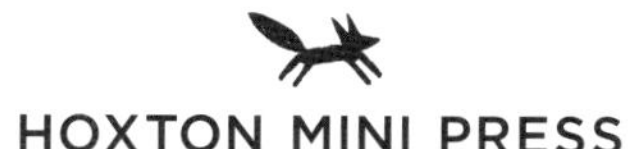

HOXTON MINI PRESS

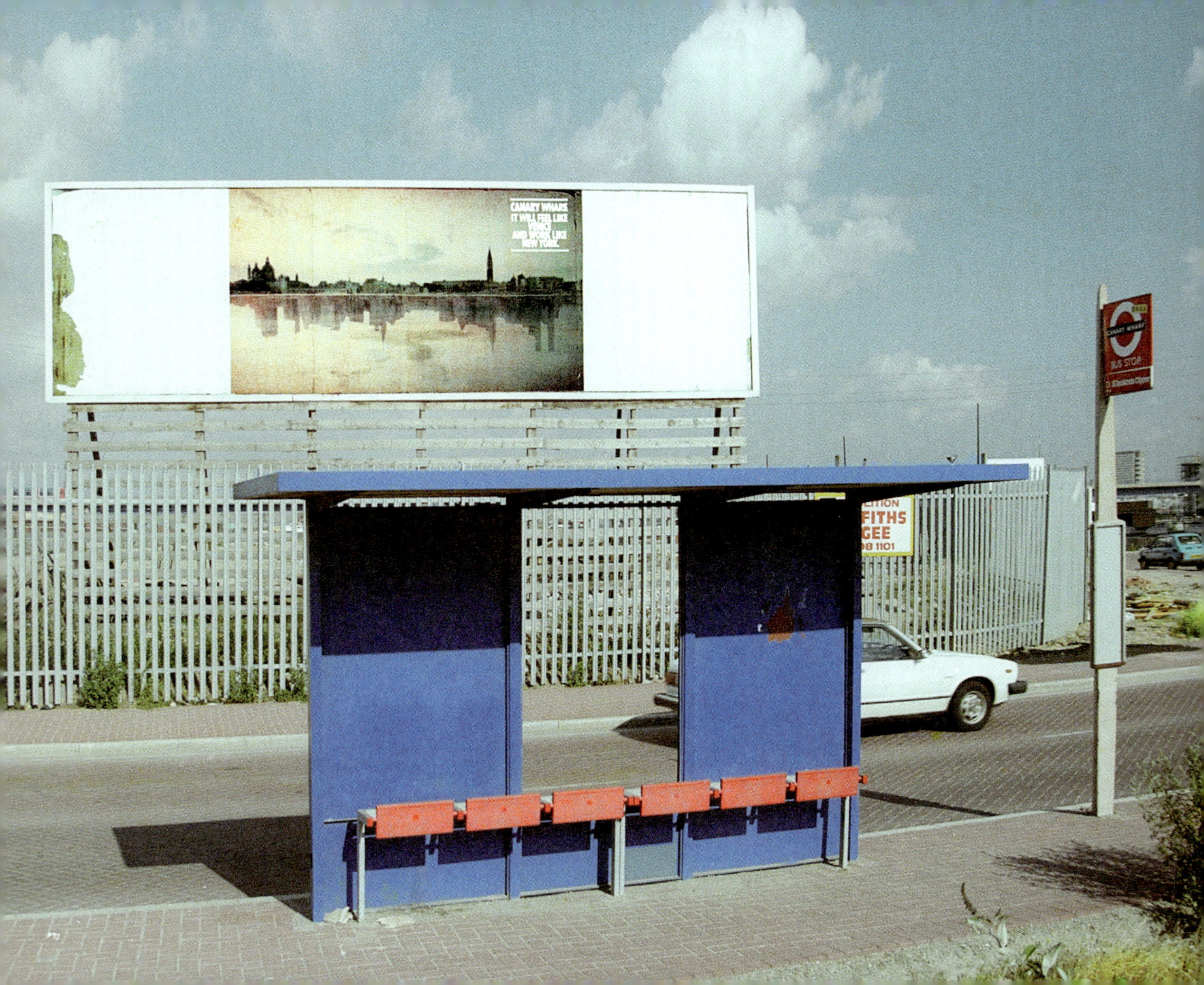
CANARY WHARF
IT WILL FEEL LIKE
VENICE
AND WORK LIKE
NEW YORK.
BUS STOP
FITHS
GEE
8 1101

INTRODUCTION

Created during his spare time whilst driving underground trains for a living, Tim Brown's previously unpublished photographs stand as a unique and fascinating glimpse into one of London's most radical periods of transformation.

Tim's photos – presented here as if following a train journey navigating the further reaches of East London and heading towards the centre of town – emerged on Flickr about 10 years ago during the first flush of social media photo repositories. They represent a prodigious photographic survey of the clearance of the world's largest dockland complex and creation of a new transport system forming the foundations of regeneration and renewal.

His deadpan urban landscapes combine a cinematic scope with an elegy for a fast-disappearing world, a world of physical toil, industry, invention, drink and ordinary life about to be replaced – with almost indecent haste – into offices and dormitories for those employed in the service and financial economy.

A note about treatment of the original materials:

Almost all of Tim Brown's pictures in this book were shot on Kodacolor negative film with a Pentax 35mm camera. The selected frames were re-photographed on a lightbox using a high-resolution camera. This method, as opposed to conventional scanning, preserves the subtle, dynamic range of the 35mm film originals.

Consulting closely with Tim about the preparation of his negatives for reproduction, I have made a few minor perspective corrections to avoid converging vertical lines and some lens aberrations at the edges of wide-angle images. This has made some cropping necessary and as a result the images are 5:4 ratio instead of 3:2 which would be normal for 35mm frames. Aside from that, these pictures are unmanipulated.

Chris Dorley-Brown, London, 2019

Opposite page: The billboard reads 'Canary Wharf: it will feel like Venice and work like New York', Westferry Circus, 1987

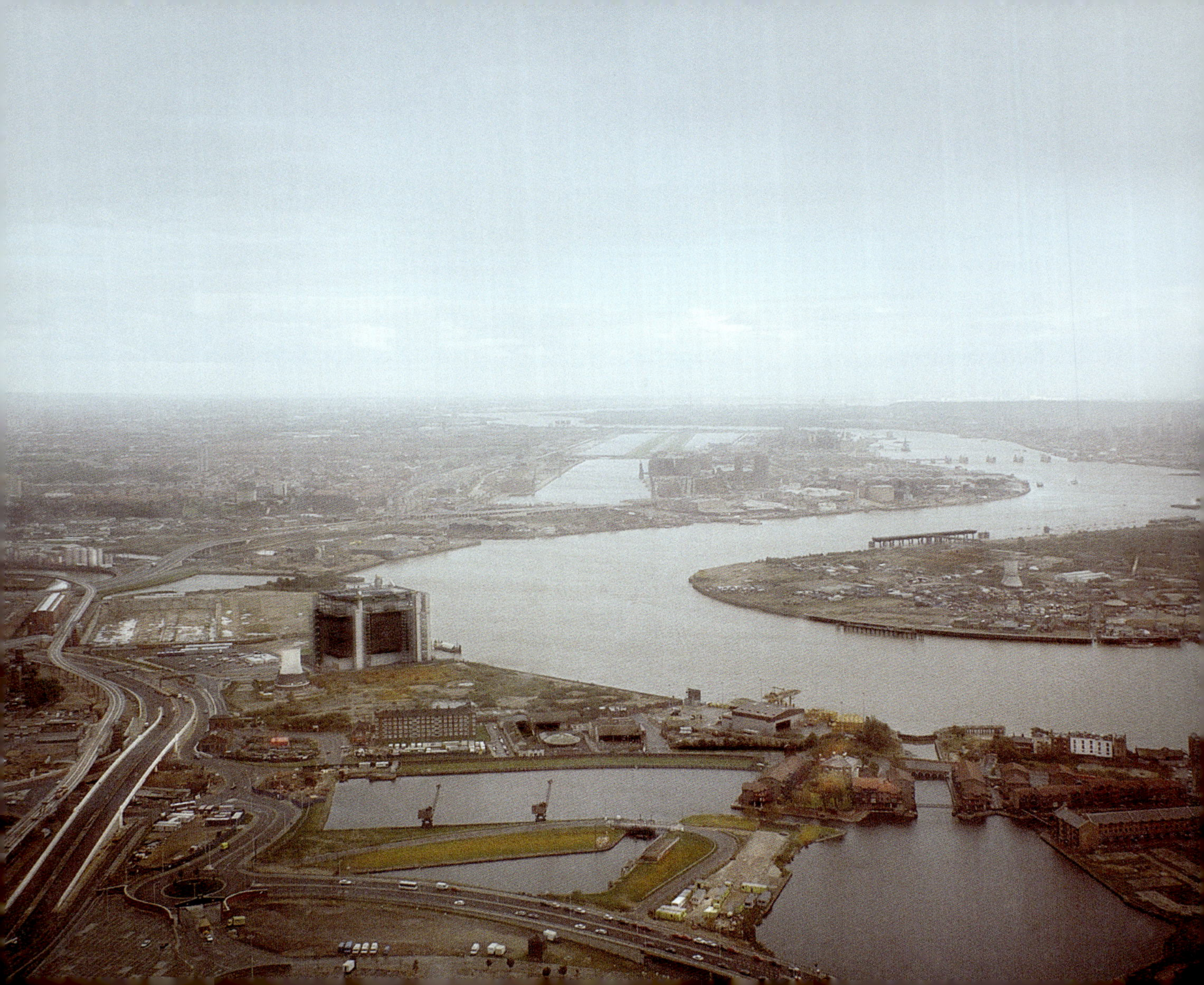

IN CONVERSATION: TIM BROWN

Chris Dorley-Brown So, Tim, you were driving Underground trains on the Central Line during the time you were making these pictures, right?

Tim Brown Yes, I joined the Underground in about 1984. I had worked for General Electric and left there to work on the Underground as a railman. After that I became a guard for a couple of years and then started as a driver around the time of the King's Cross fire in 1987.

CDB Were you making photographs at that time?

TB Yes, I had made some Kodachromes between 1981 and 1983 and in 1985 I moved to Leytonstone to live. I started shooting on colour negative after a couple of years' break from photography.

CDB I have had a chance to look through your entire archive during the scanning and editing process in making this book and it seems you were concentrating exclusively on documenting a landscape that was about to change radically. Was that the purpose of the pictures?

TB I was interested in seeing this new transport project from scratch [the Docklands Light Railway]. I went to some public meetings and it seemed that the DLR was designed as a test bed for a cheaper transport system and that maybe the Underground was going to go that way as well with driverless trains and less staff, everything being automated.

CDB I'm so glad you were making these pictures – they are a rare documentation of this strange, miniature railway system seemingly being built in the middle of a desert landscape.

TB It was a very tightly budgeted railway as I don't think anyone was sure it was going to be used but as soon as Canary Wharf started to get built it created

Opposite page: Looking east from the 50th floor of Canary Wharf

a momentum, so they practically rebuilt it and extended it. The land at West India Quay had a negative land value but once the DLR started to go in, the value then started to scroll into the millions. It's why smelly old Billingsgate Market was pushed out of the city to there and now I think there are plans to push them out of this place too. There's millions to be made under all that fish.

CDB Did you think that by taking these photographs you were preserving a world that was going to disappear?

TB Yes, I thought it was going to be swept away but I didn't imagine the extent of the change that was going to happen. For instance, who would have imagined that 'Fortress Wapping' (Rupert Murdoch's News International) would be demolished so soon to make way for expensive housing? It was difficult to spot what was going to be valuable for the future, so I took a scattergun approach in my surveys of places to try and get everything but I was limited by the film I could afford. And there was no instant review with this sort of analogue technolo-gy, I had to wait for the post! I also had to physically find these things in the first place; there was no Google or tourist guides to the desert of Docklands, just some artists' dreams about the megacity to come.

CDB So, were you photographing on days off or between shifts driving trains?

TB I was working late shifts mostly so I would go out on a quick survey in the mornings. The Docklands pictures were done at weekends because I had to do a lot of walking; there was hardly any public transport. In fact, there was nothing there at all, nothing going on apart from films being made, like Stanley Kubrick's *Full Metal Jacket* and Derek Jarman was doing things down at West India Docks, also Jean-Michel Jarre had a huge open-air show at Millennium Mills in Silvertown.

CDB Not forgetting *The Long Good Friday*!

TB That was Heron Quays and Canary Wharf! Yes, in fact, I was looking for the locations of *The Long*

Good Friday when I made these pictures.

CDB You photographed the set of *Full Metal Jacket* in Beckton quite extensively. It was the old gasworks in Beckton and Kubrick managed to get hold of it and recreate the Tet Offensive of the Vietnam War amongst the concrete buildings. They let him blow the hell out of it, destroy what was left… it was because he hated flying and didn't want to shoot it in Vietnam.

TB Yes, just after they finished filming, the palm trees ended up being replanted in Southend, so something survives of it. They were going to clear the site anyway, so they blew it up for the film.

CDB The picture from the 50th floor of Canary Wharf looking east [see previous spread] shows how barren the landscape is.

TB Shortly after I took that picture they closed the building to the public.

CDB If you took a picture from the same place now, you would only see other skyscrapers blocking your view, it has completely transformed. Some of the new buildings you have photographed in the Canary Wharf area have already been demolished.

TB I wanted to get pictures of the new buildings while they were shiny and new!

CDB How old were you when you did these pictures?

TB I was 27 in 1987, when many of the photos were taken.

CDB Were you looking at other photographers' work or pictures of London?

TB Not really, there was no internet back then though I did buy a few books and I went to the occasional exhibition at Hamiltons Gallery in the West End. They were mostly black and white pictures. These didn't affect how I wanted to photograph things; I wanted to develop my own style, in colour, using a straightforward approach.

CDB I think it's a similar approach that David Granick adopted, whose work was published as a forerunner to your book [*The East End in Colour 1960–1980*], the same territory and a similar style of documenting a place undergoing transformation. You were both anticipating forthcoming changes in East London's landscape, both pursuing a mission to preserve, in a way. Though in Granick's day there seemed to be no vision presented to people of how things may develop to make their lives better. It was like a landscape being rundown deliberately, left to rot. But a decade later, when you took over his role, there appears to be a masterplan in place.

TB In the image of what is now Westferry Circus [see opposite Introduction page], there is a billboard opposite a bus shelter which shows a fantasy photomontage with the slogan 'Canary Wharf: it will feel like Venice and work like New York'. I was standing on a pile of rubble in the middle of a wasteland when I took that picture and I was thinking how absurd the vision was and how unlikely it was to come true. But I suppose it has come true, in a way, and bizarrely the Twin Towers are shown upside down – a weird prophecy, maybe? And of course there was a huge bombing near this spot shortly after the buildings were completed.

CDB Does your family have roots in the East End?

TB On my mother's side, yes, two were dock workers in the Royal Docks, a ship's carpenter and a clerk. On her side there are Krakow origins and some Huguenots. My father's uncle was a Welshman, he was a nightwatchman at Dunster Castle and a councillor involved in championing Butlin's in Minehead. My paternal grandfather was a ship's steward out of Southampton and my father was magazine editor of *Hi-Fi News*. My mum is still alive. She grew up in Manor Park and Forest Gate.

CDB Another place you shot many pictures was Leytonstone, before the M11 was built.

TB I was living there at the time. I knew the protests against the motorway were not going to get it stopped. I wasn't happy about it but there you go.

CDB There is a photo of a car flattened by bricks…

TB There was a severe storm and a wall fell on a row of parked cars. It was on the proposed route of the motorway.

CDB Were you still on the Underground at this point?

TB Yes, but it was getting stressful. When they introduced one-man operated trains, they removed the guard so it was just the driver. I was doing three round trips from Ealing to Hainault in a single shift. Sometimes a shift was the last train at night and the first train of the morning, but with sleet trains that ran through the night to keep the tracks clear of ice. I used to see the graffiti artist's results. Graffiti was epidemic at the time; a lot of them got killed or injured over the years. It's the reason for painted trains now – easier to clean the spray paint off.

CDB What do you think about your pictures being published in book form?

TB Well, these pictures were never intended to be seen, they were a private record and there was no internet at the time. It was only when Flickr came along [in 2004], I thought 'Hmm… maybe somebody might want to see them'. Buried for 20 years they had started to become historic but they were very mundane at the time. I wish I had done more!

December 2018

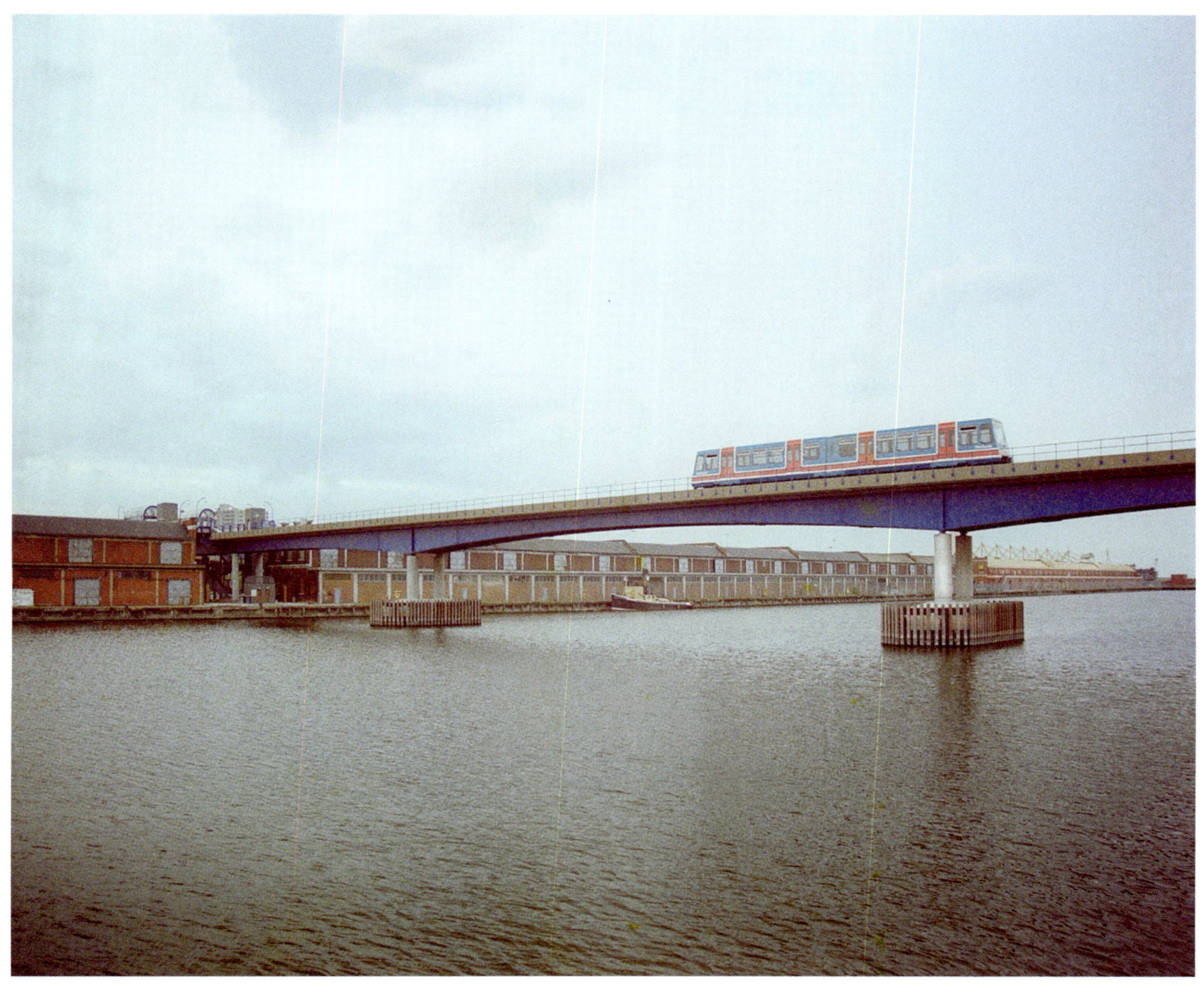

Train heading towards West India Quay DLR station, 1987

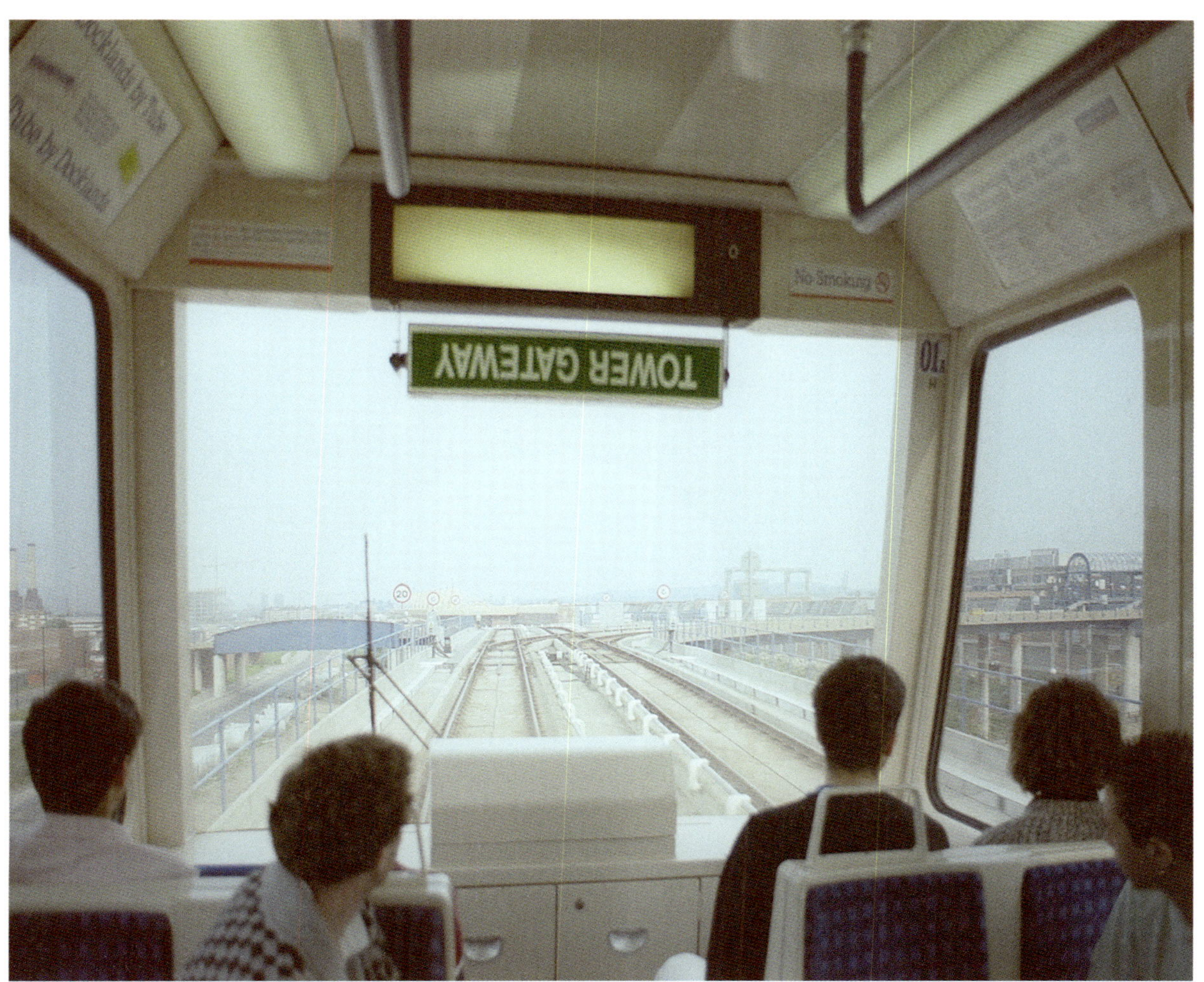

On the DLR travelling from Westferry to Poplar, 1988

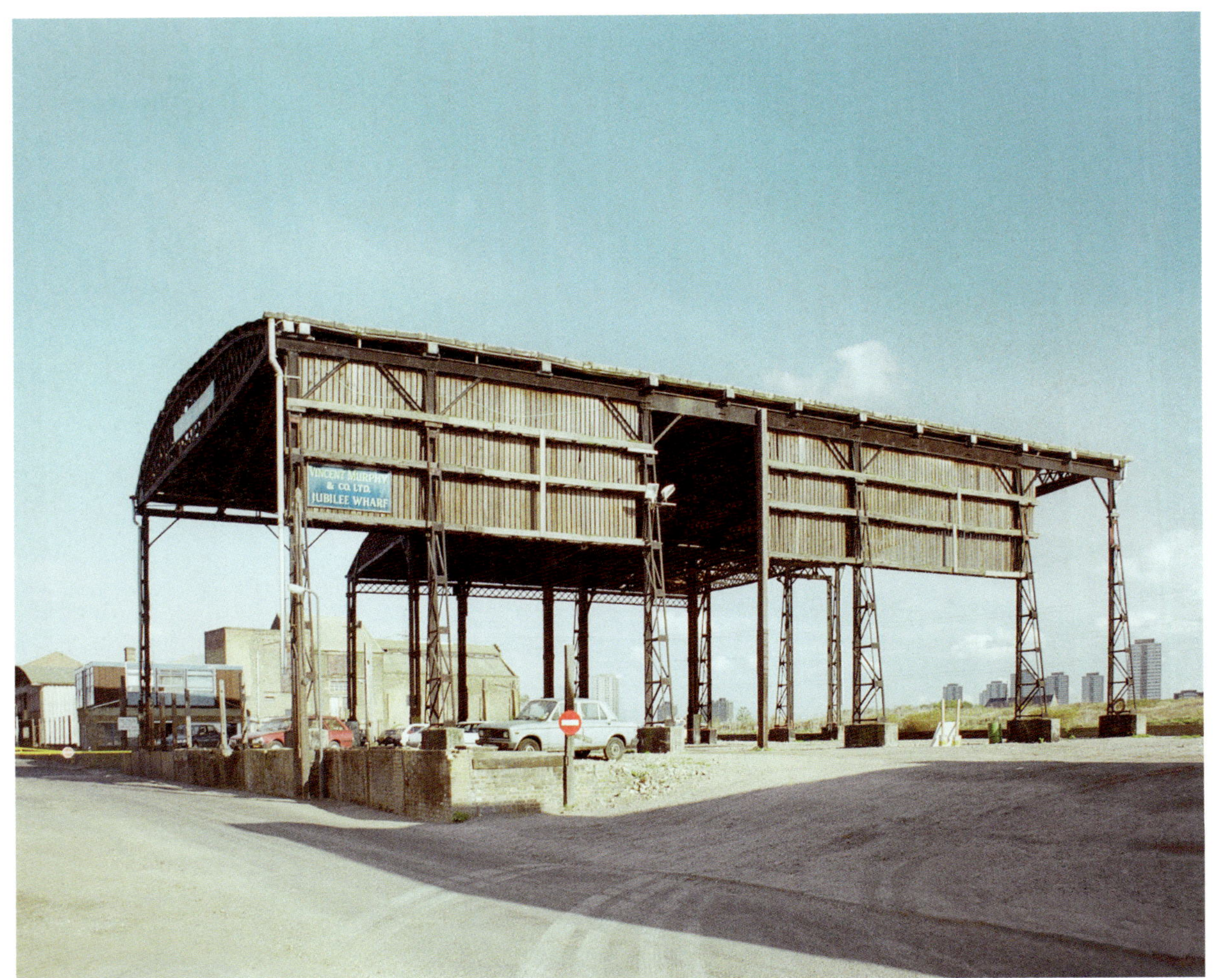

Orchard Place, 1988

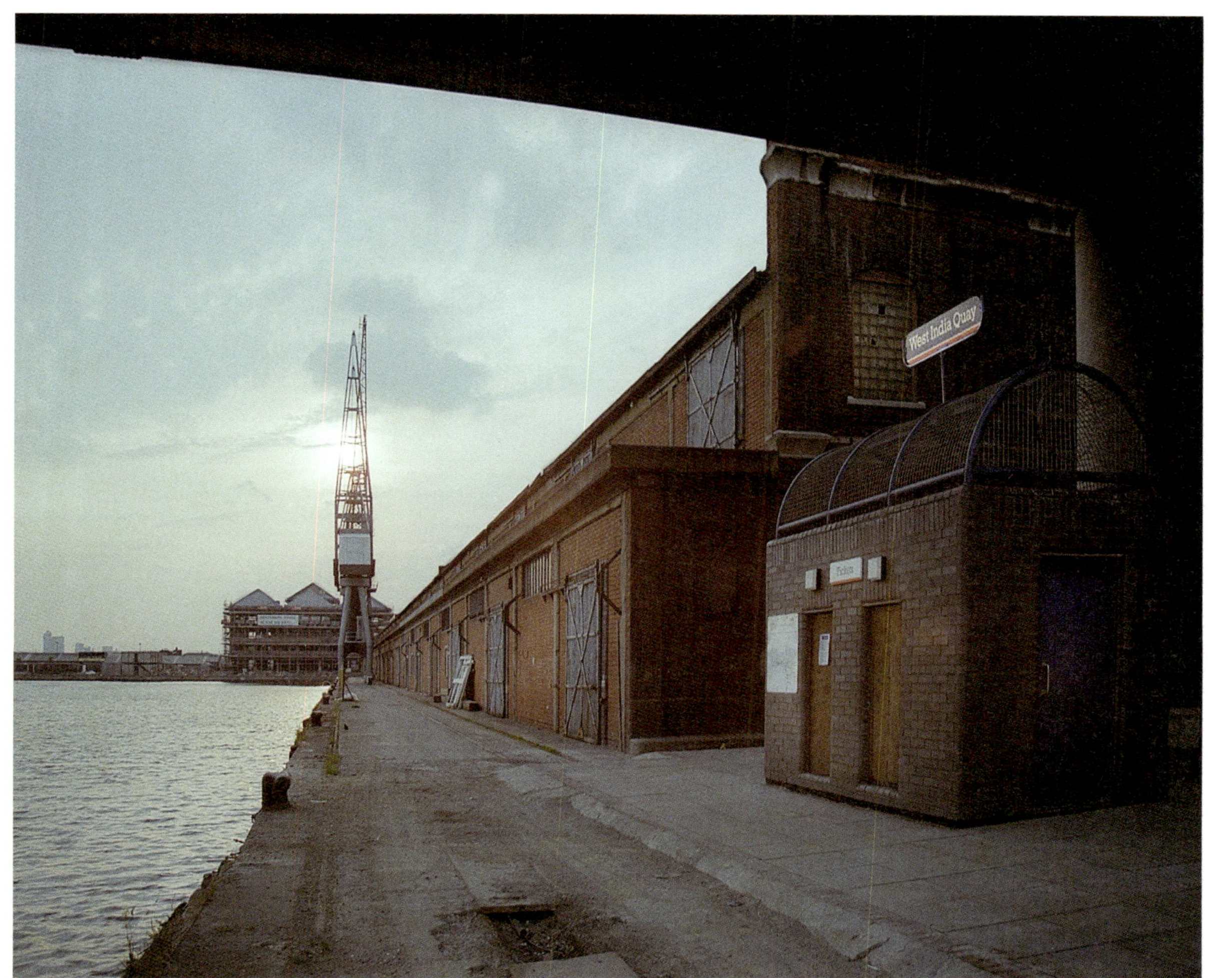

West India Quay, 1987

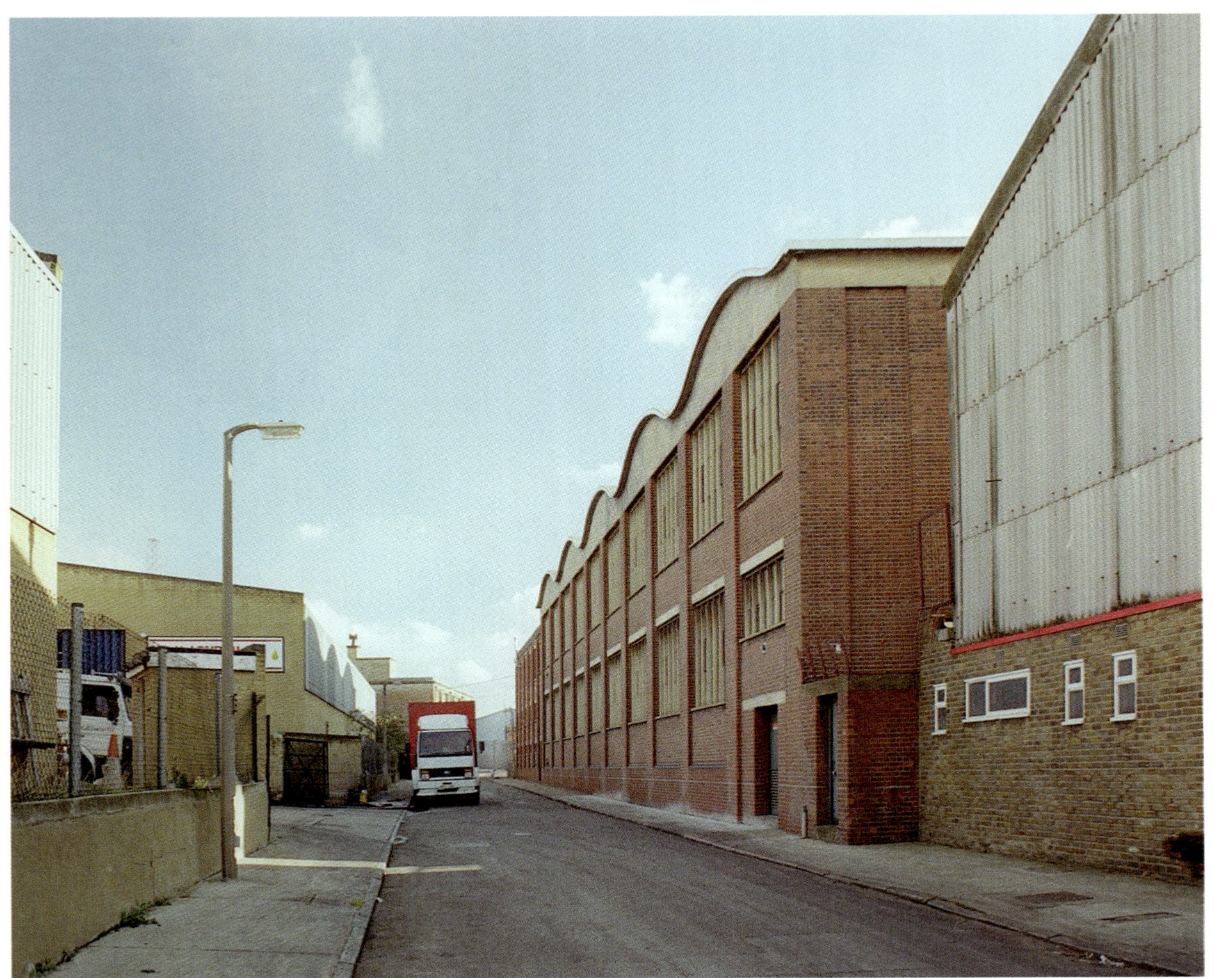

Orchard Place, 1988

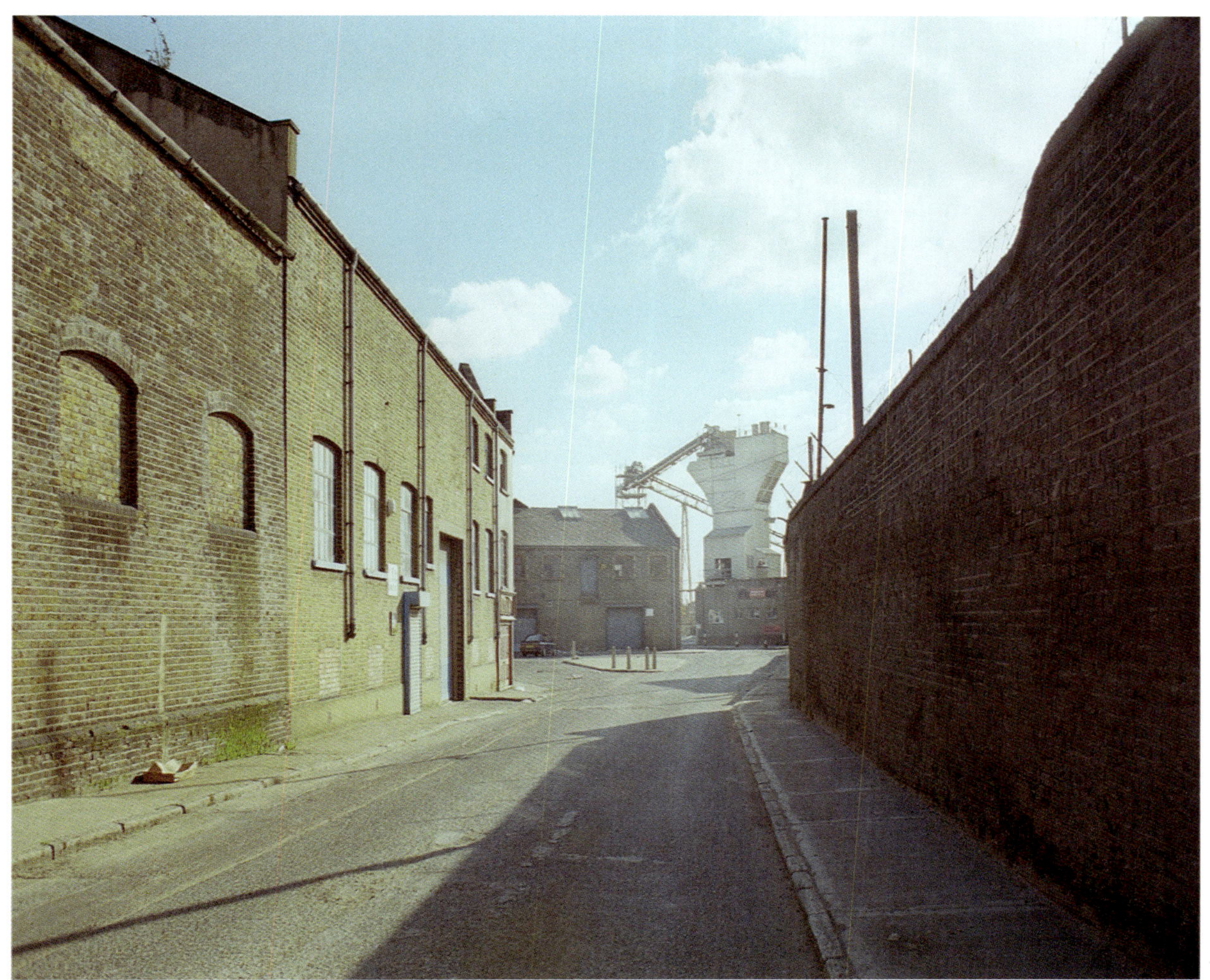
Orchard Place, 1988

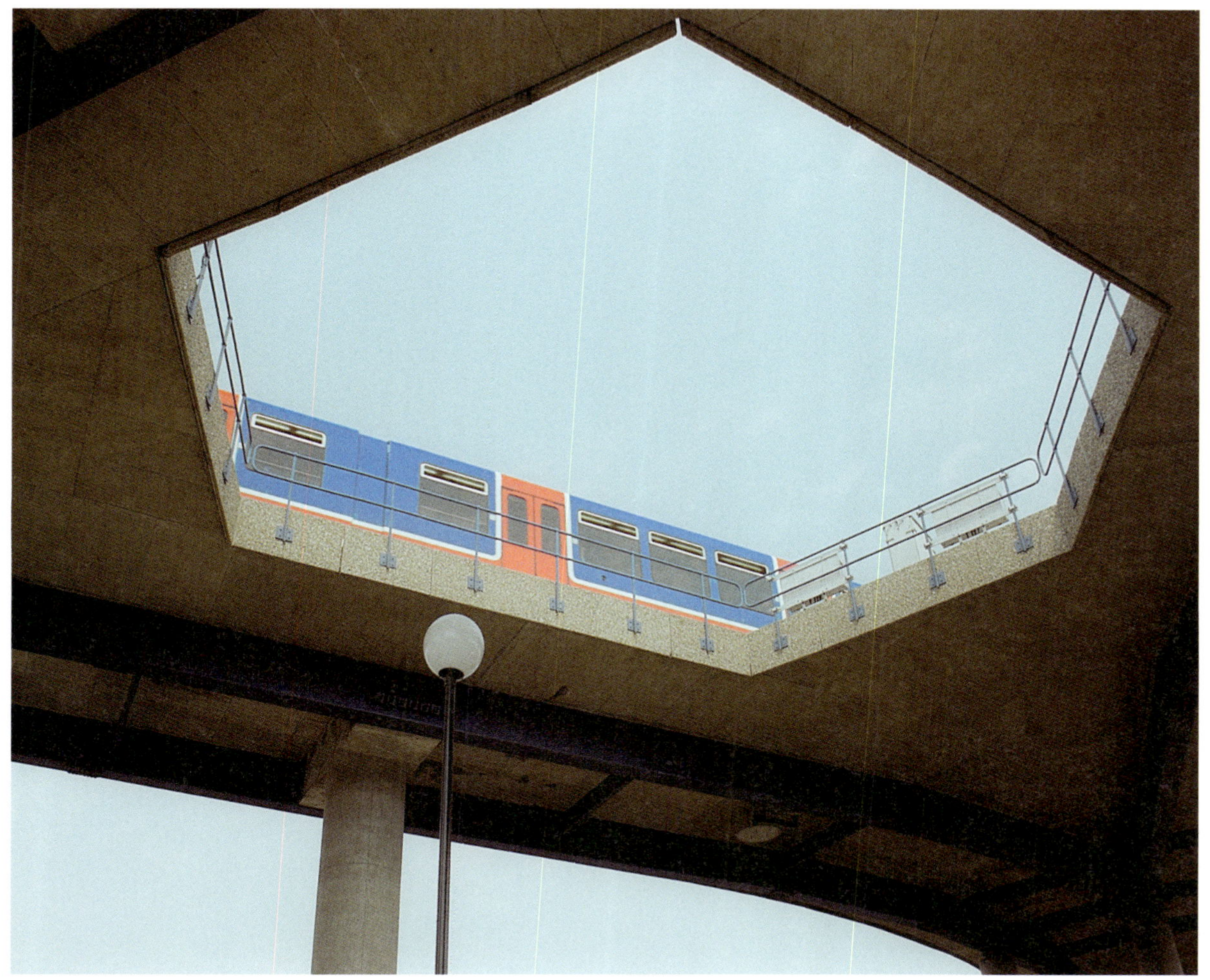

North Quay Junction, 1988

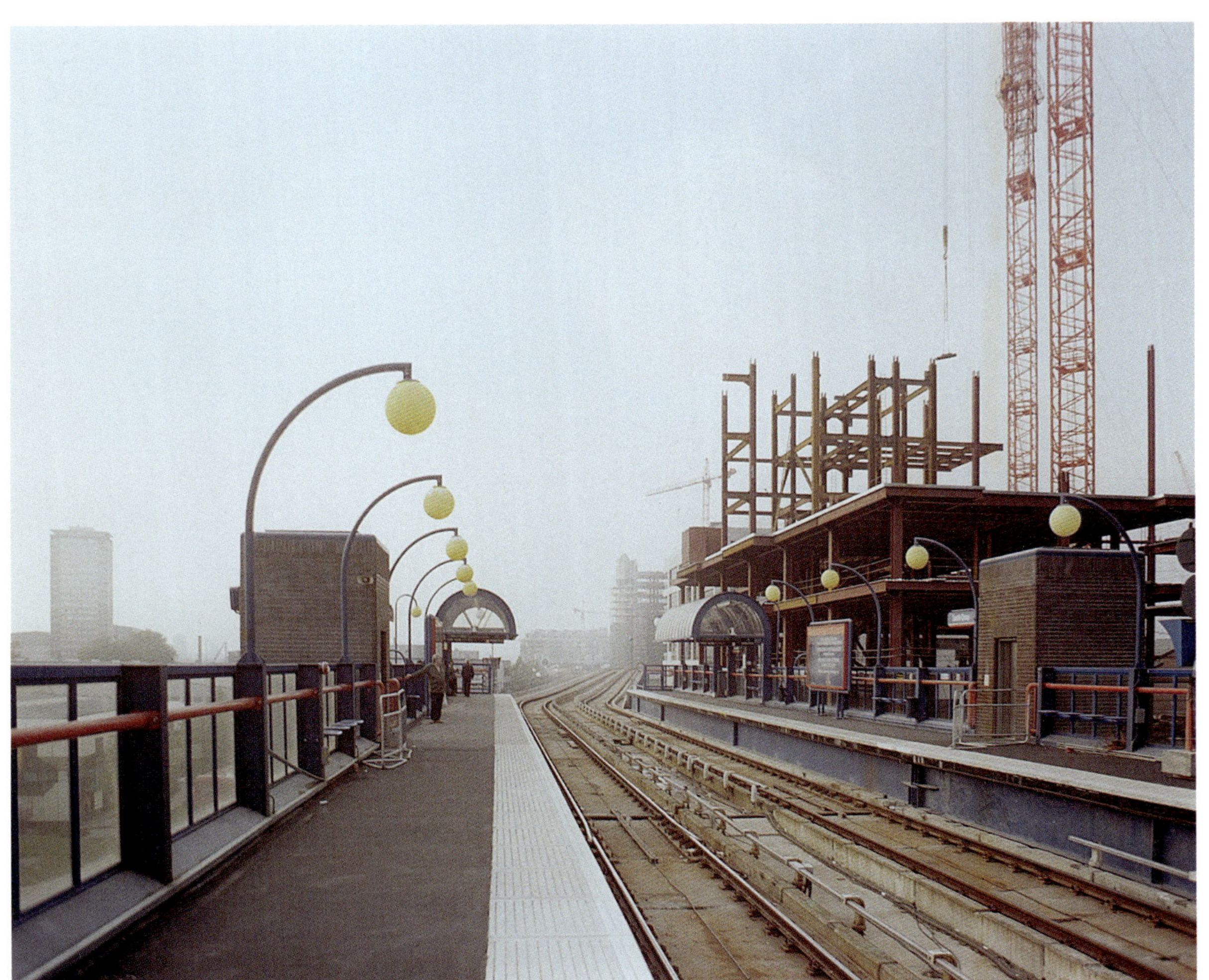

South Quay DLR station, 1989

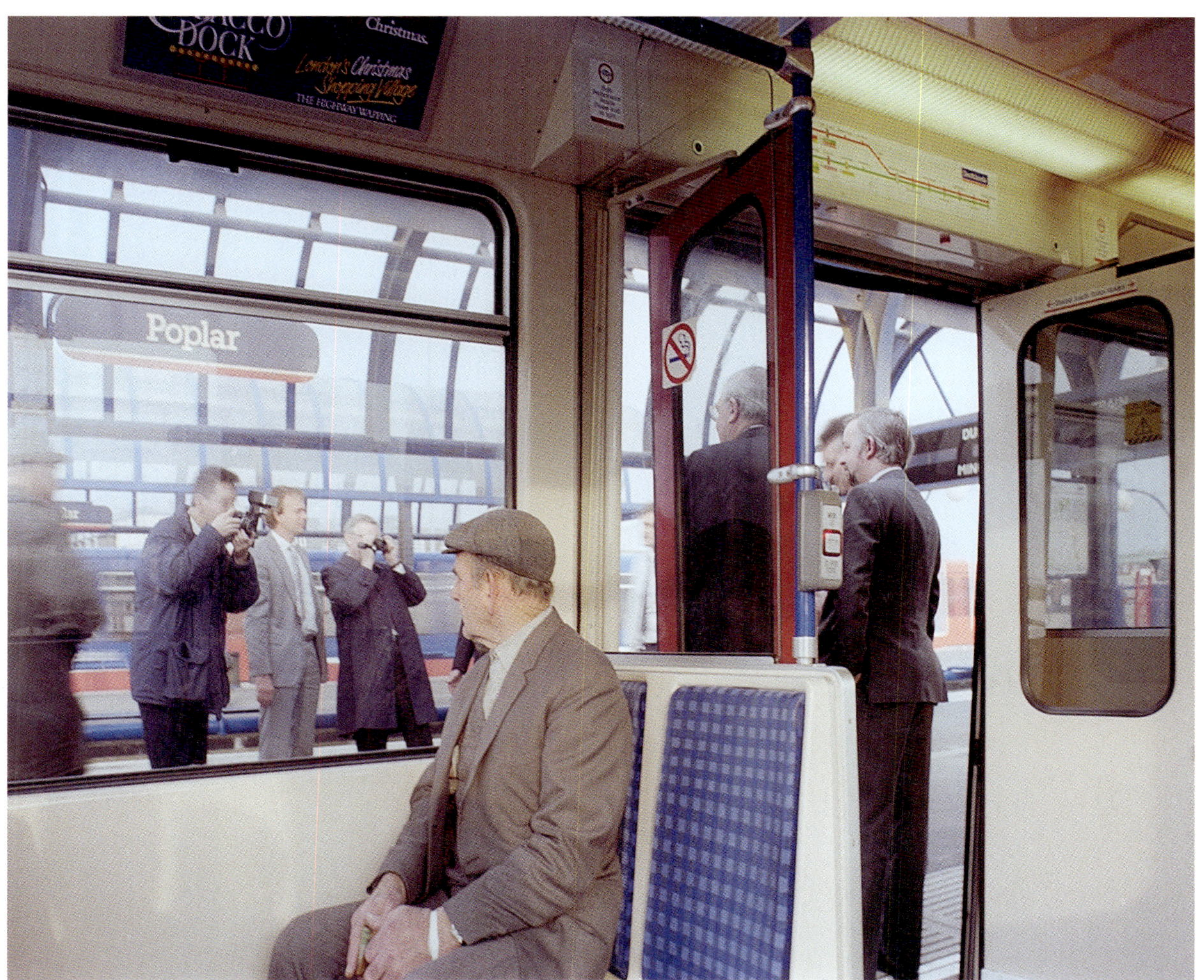

Poplar DLR station, 1989

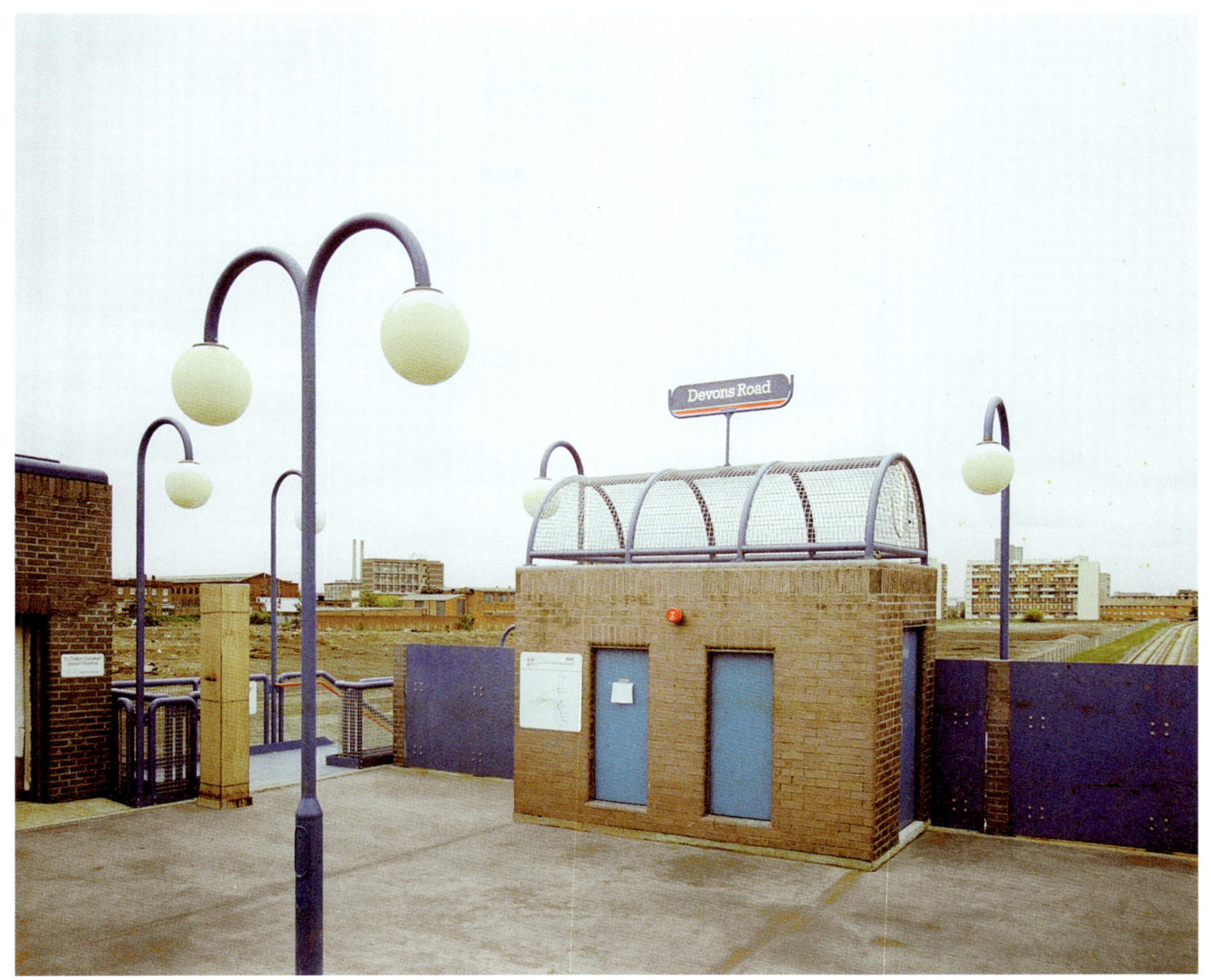

Devons Road DLR station, 1987

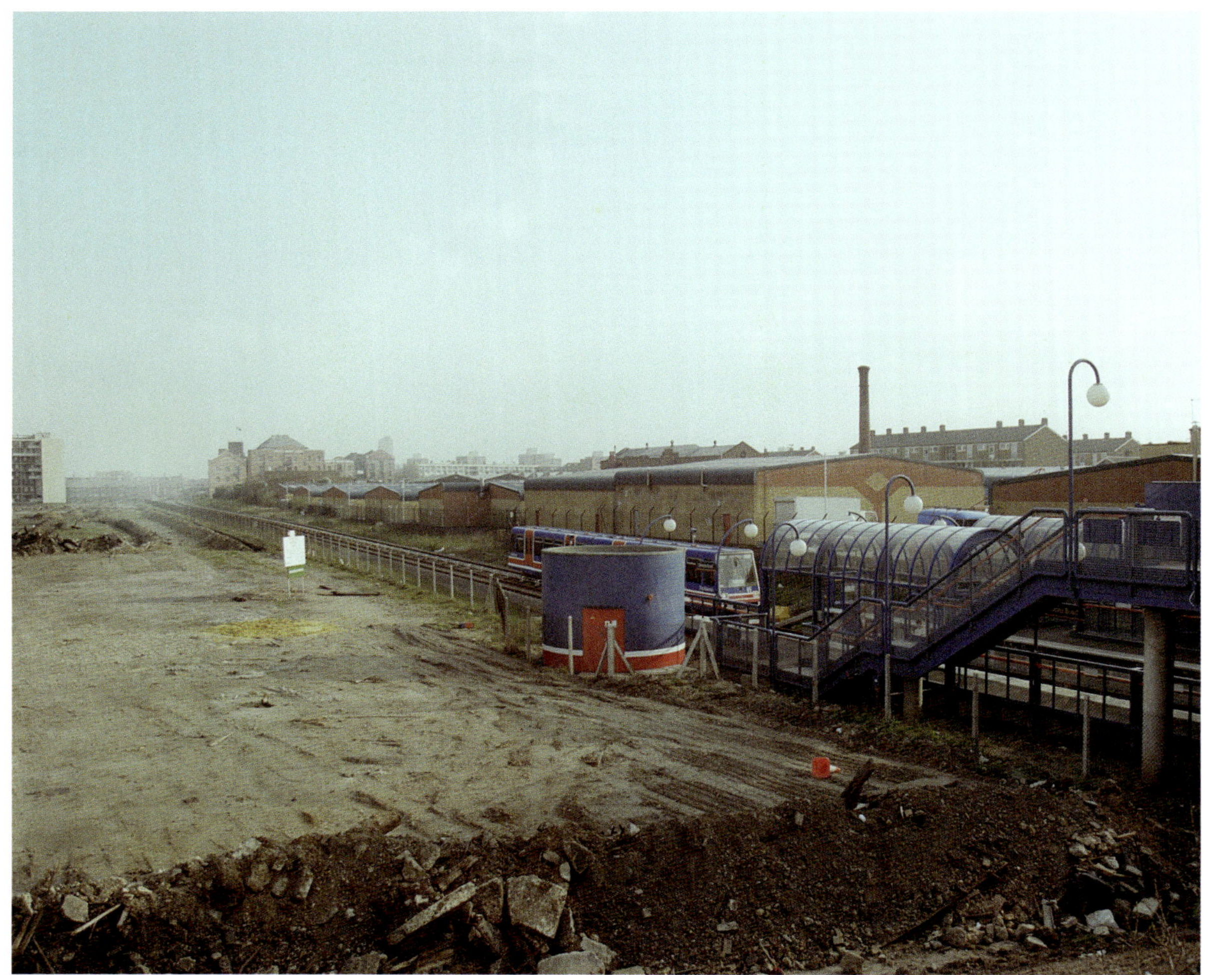

Devons Road DLR station, 1988

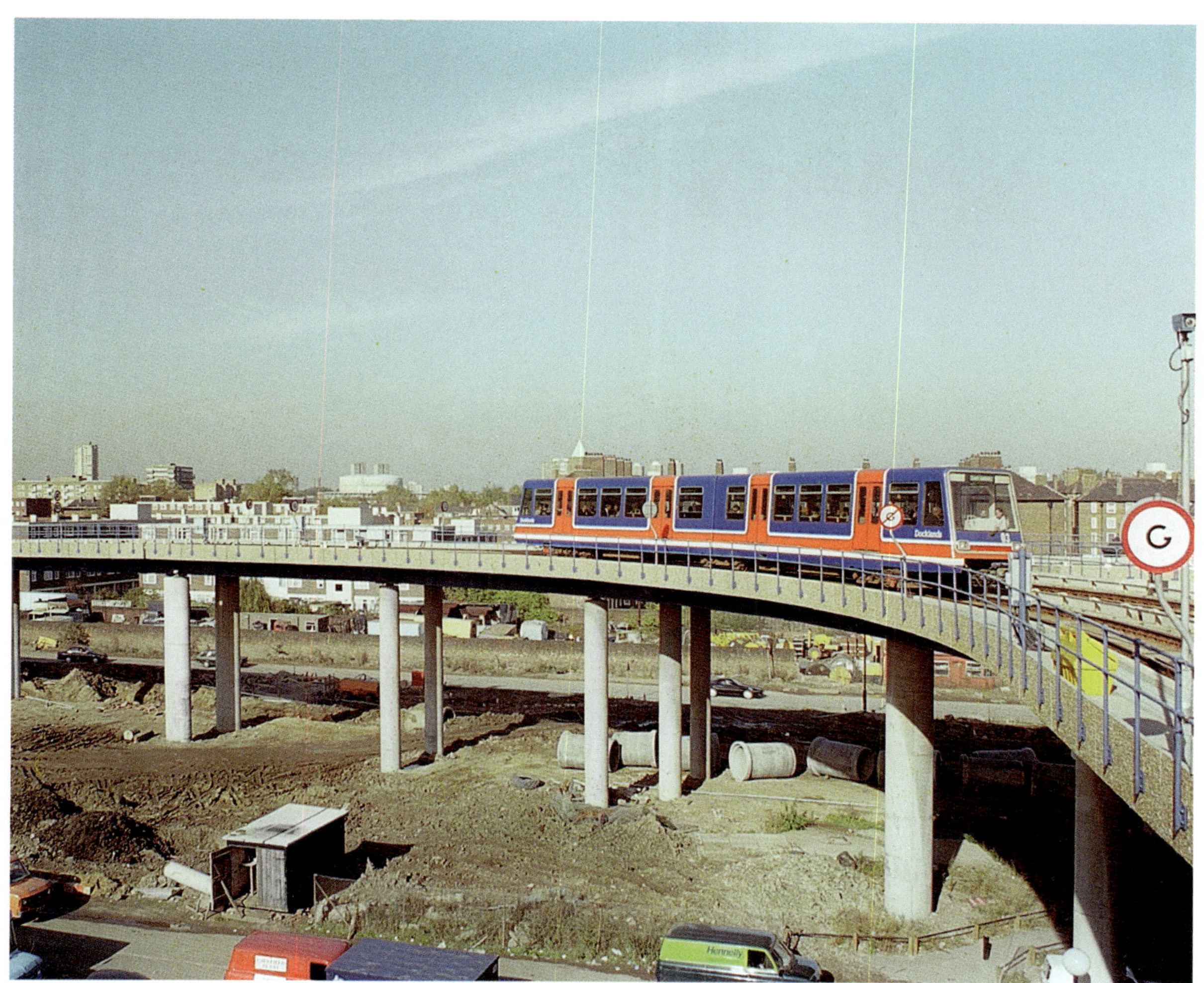

View from West India Quay DLR station, 1988

Bow Creek and Leamouth Peninsula, 1990

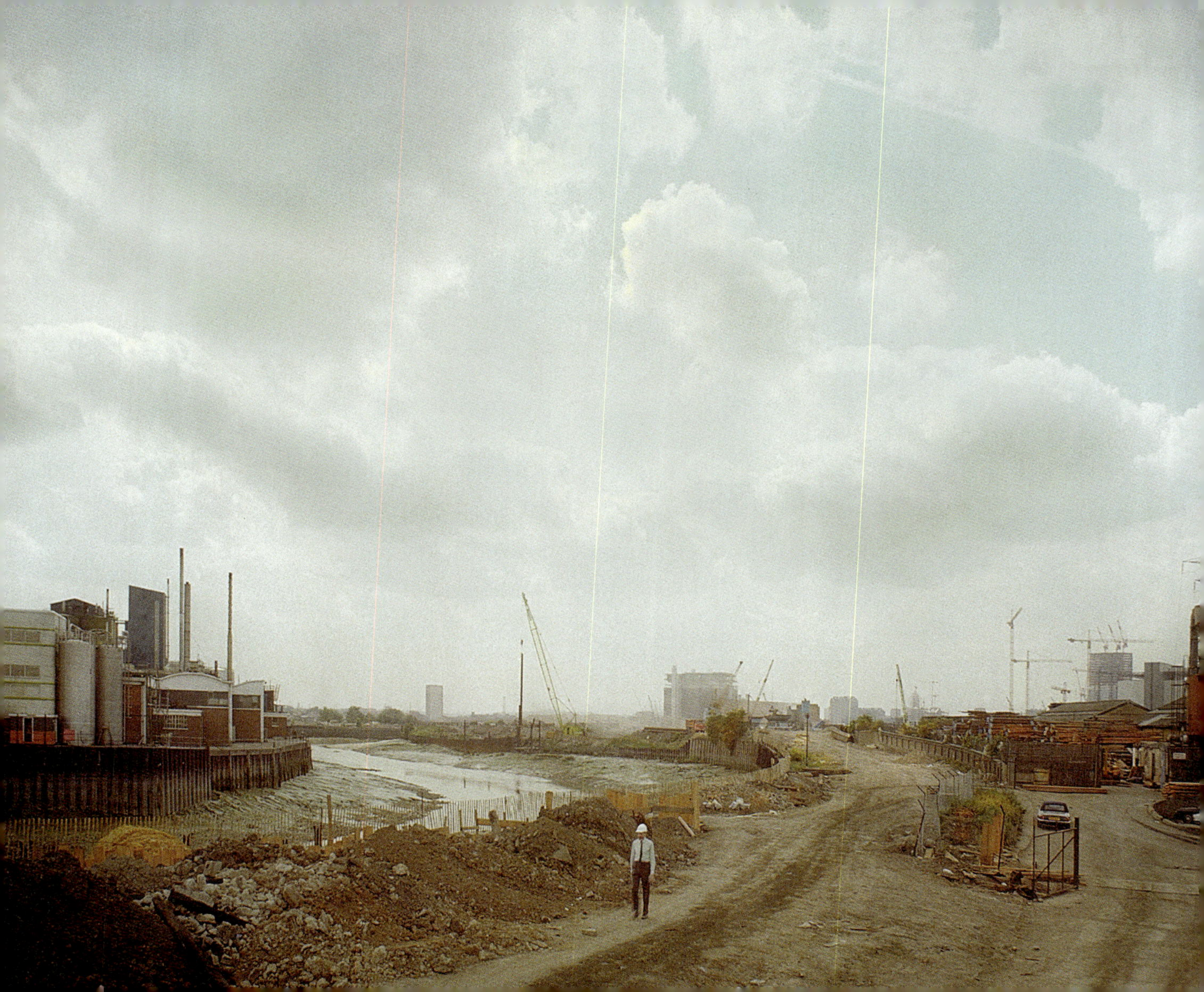

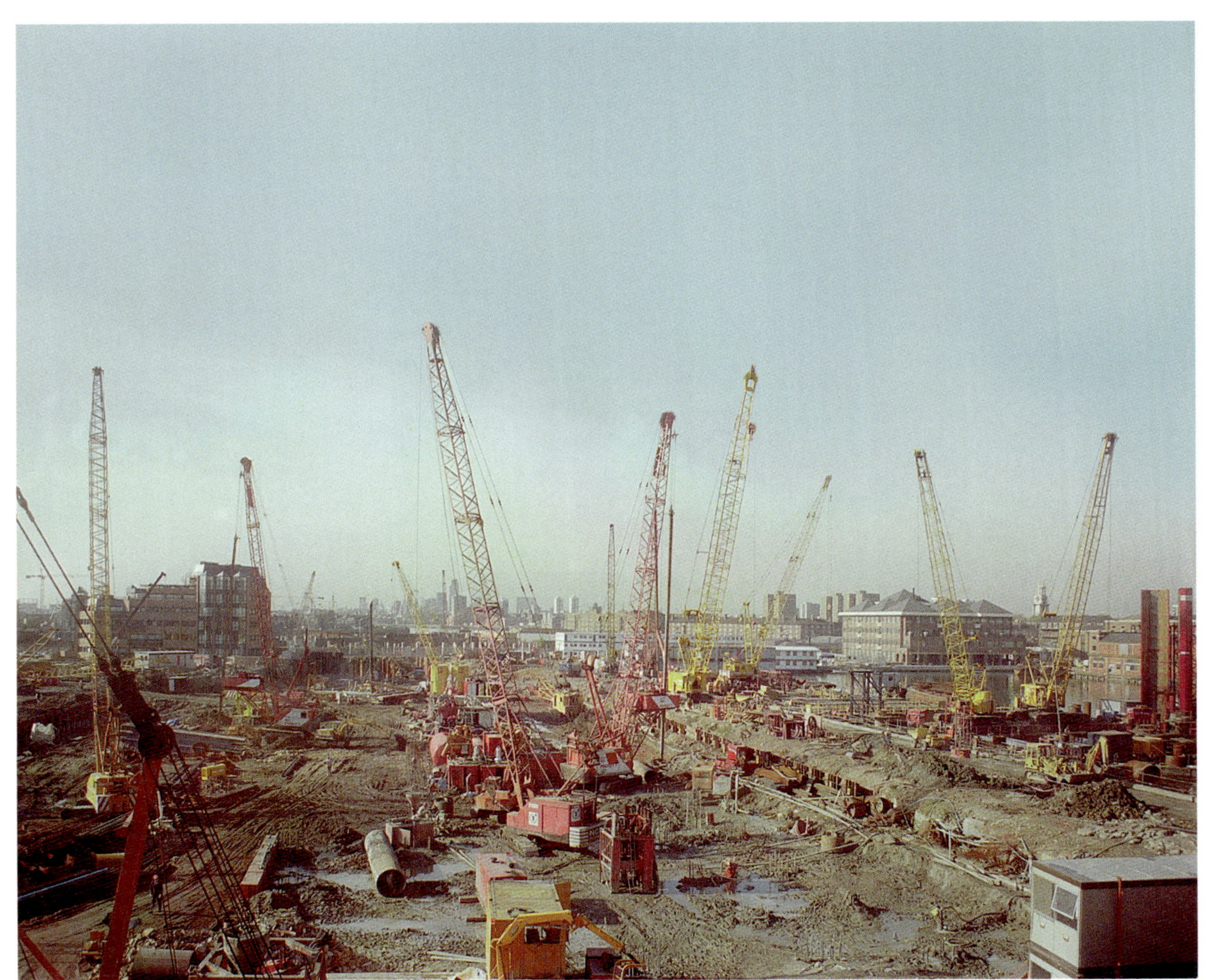

View of Canary Wharf site from Canary Wharf DLR station, 1988

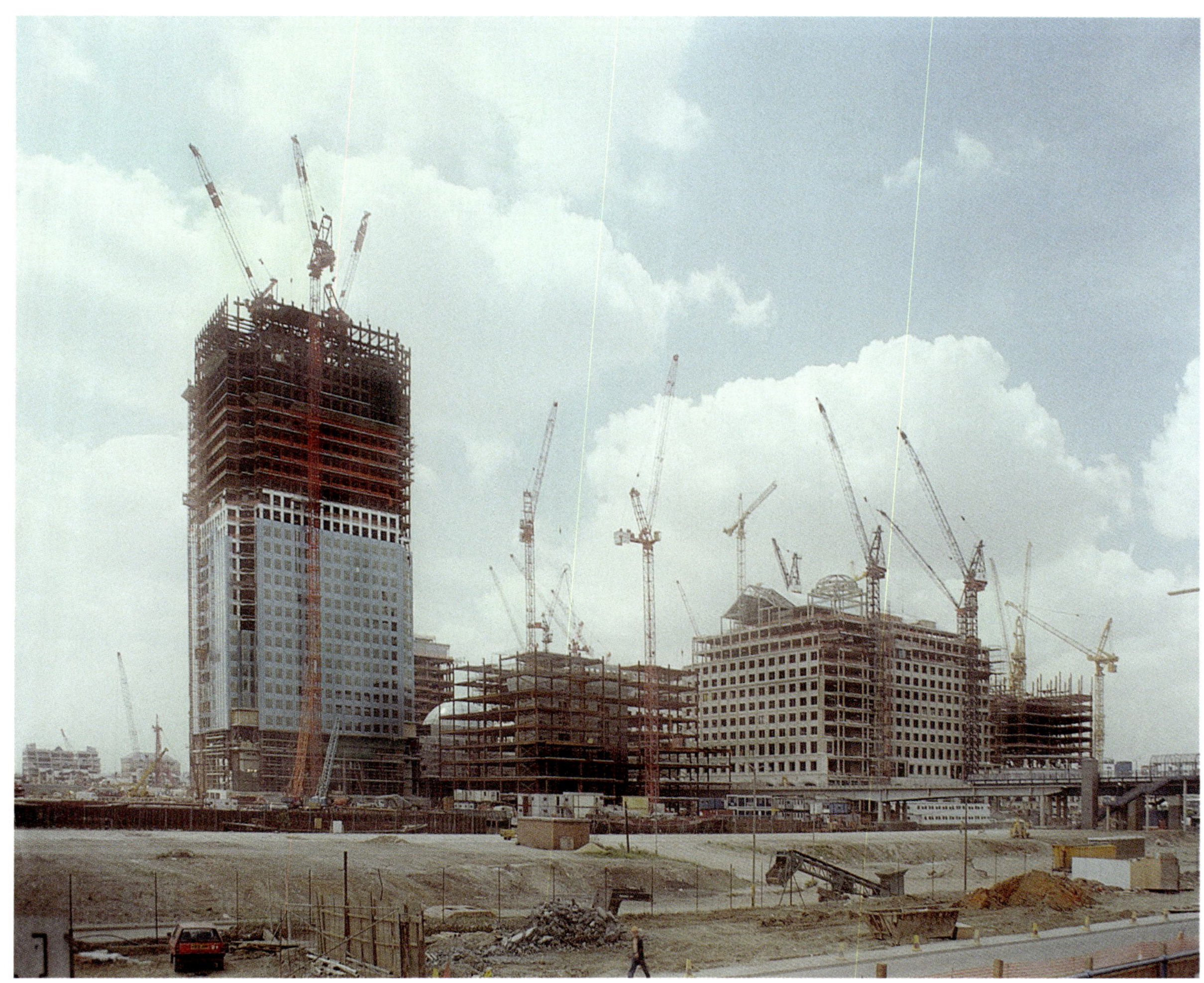

View of Canary Wharf site from Poplar DLR station, 1990

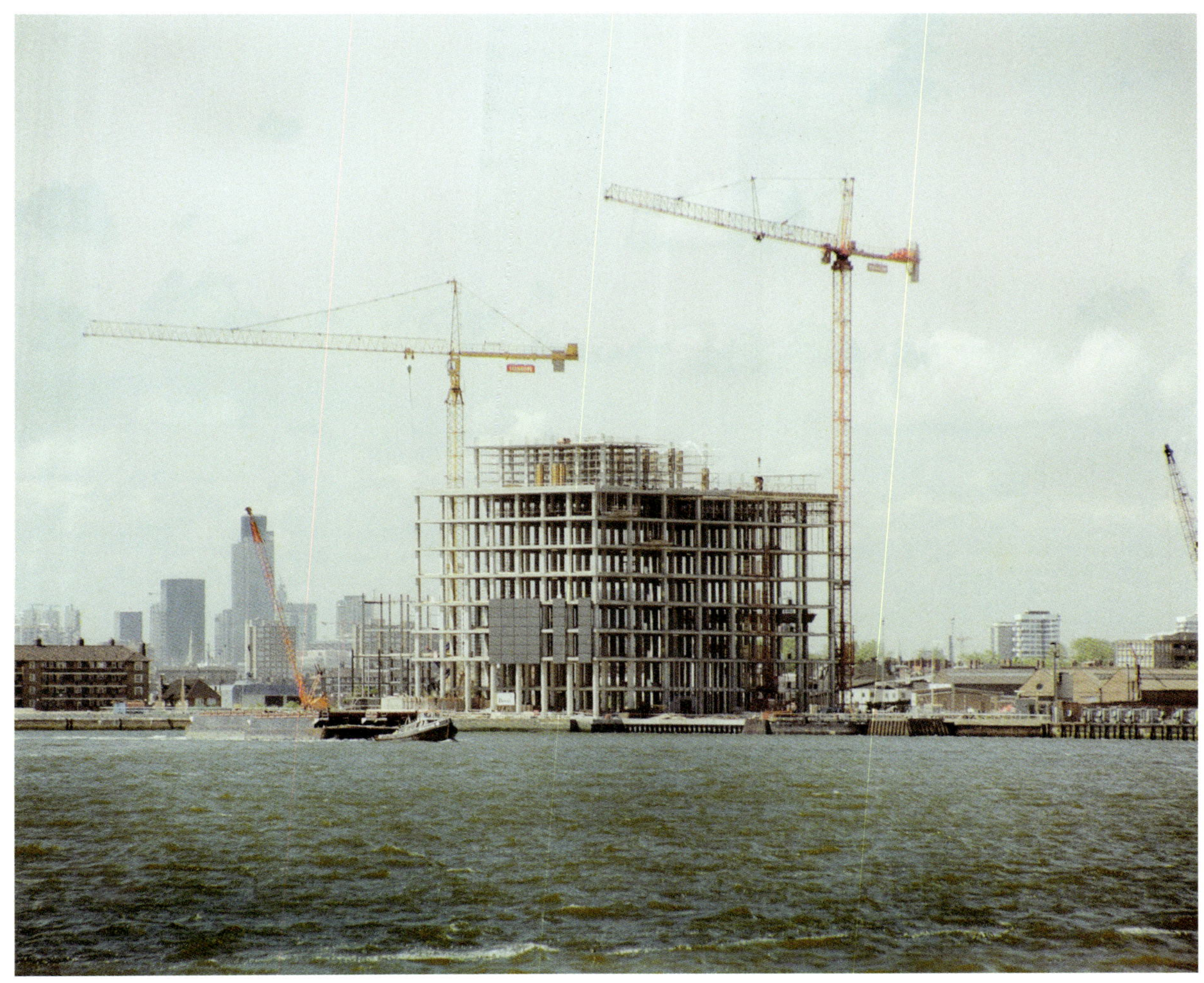

View of Reuters Data Centre, Blackwall, from Silvertown Way, 1988

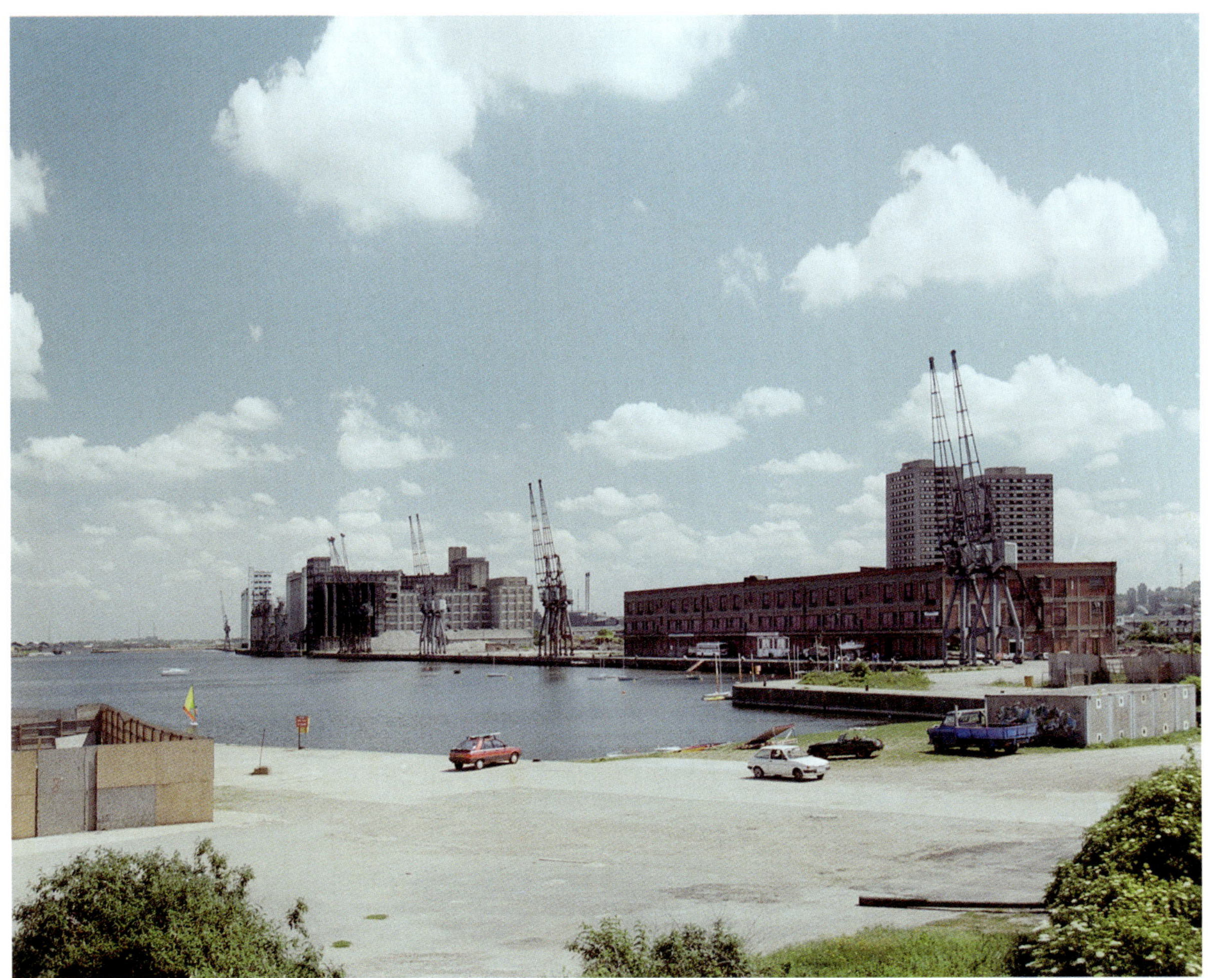

Royal Victoria Dock, 1988

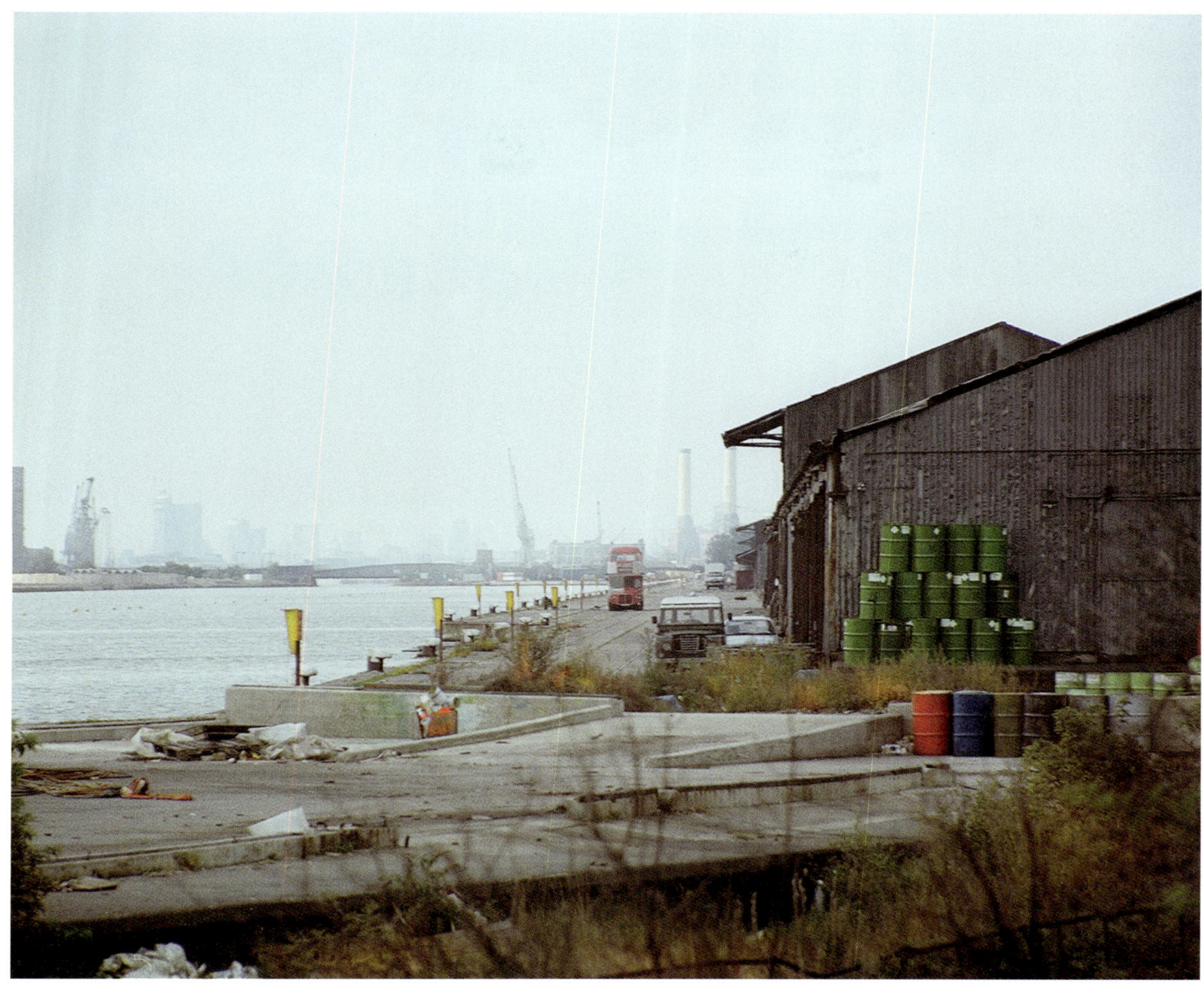

Royal Albert Dock, 1987

Set location for Stanley Kubrick's *Full Metal Jacket*, Beckton Gas Works, 1987

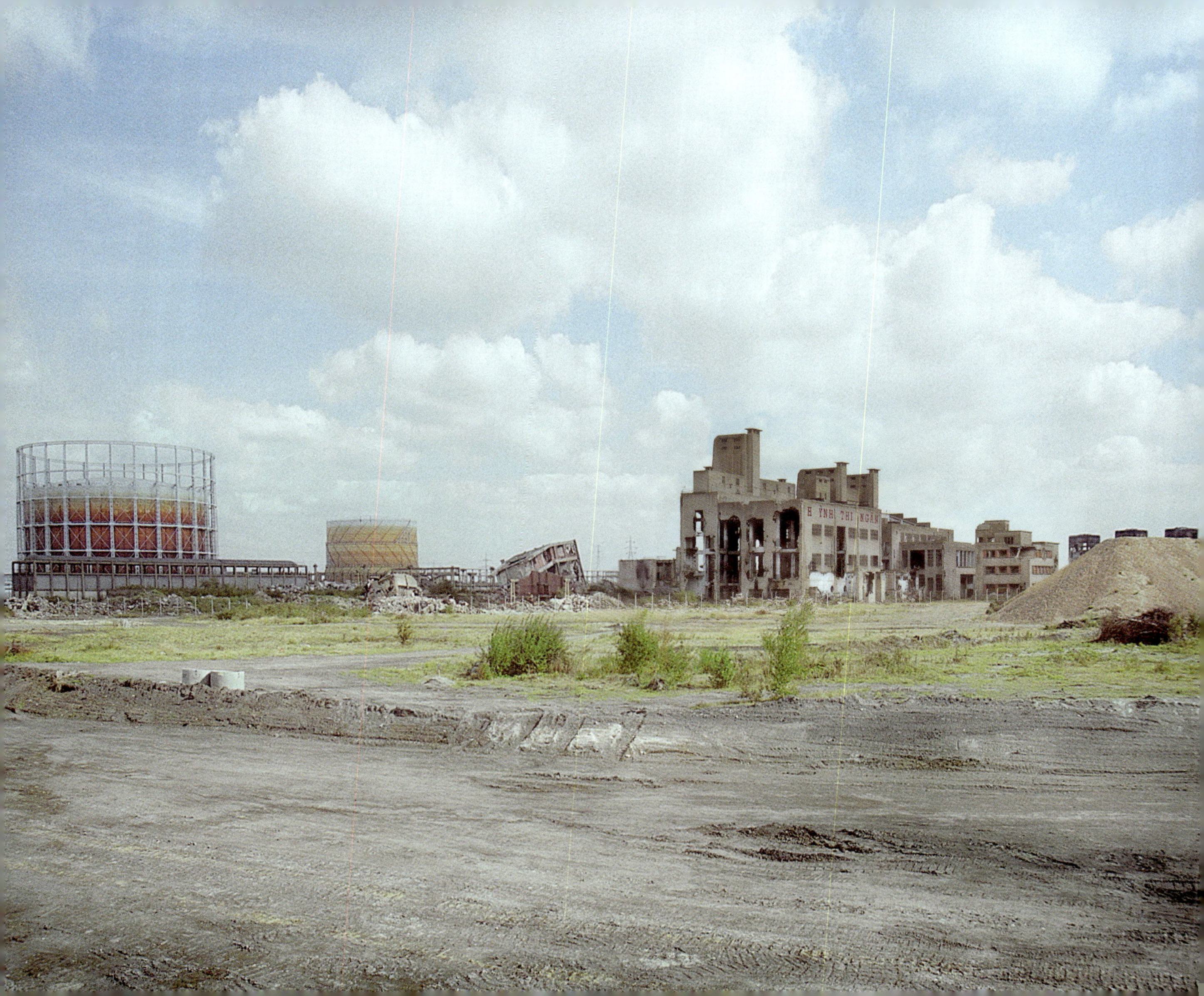
H YNH THI NGAN

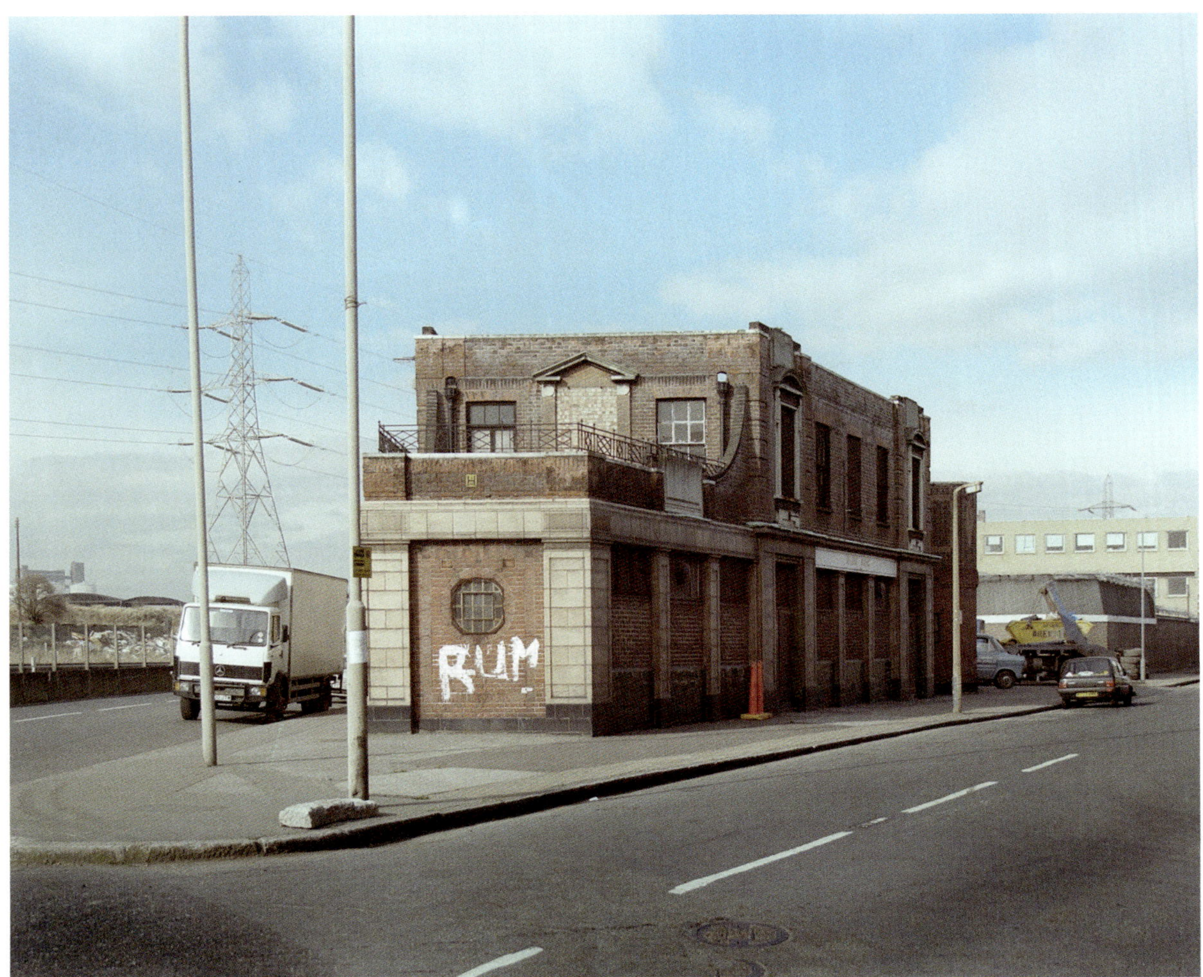

Peto Street North, 1988

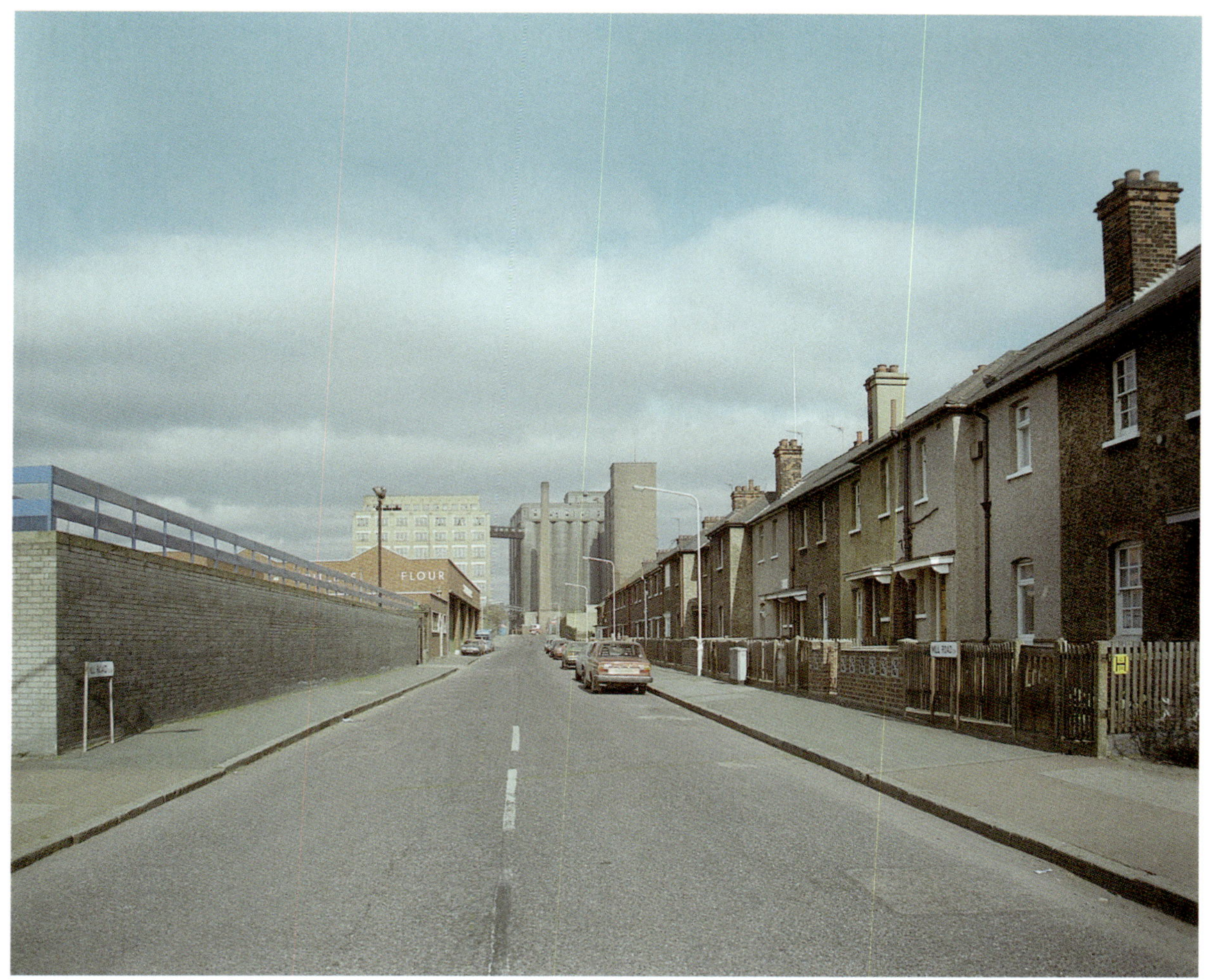

Mill Road, 1988

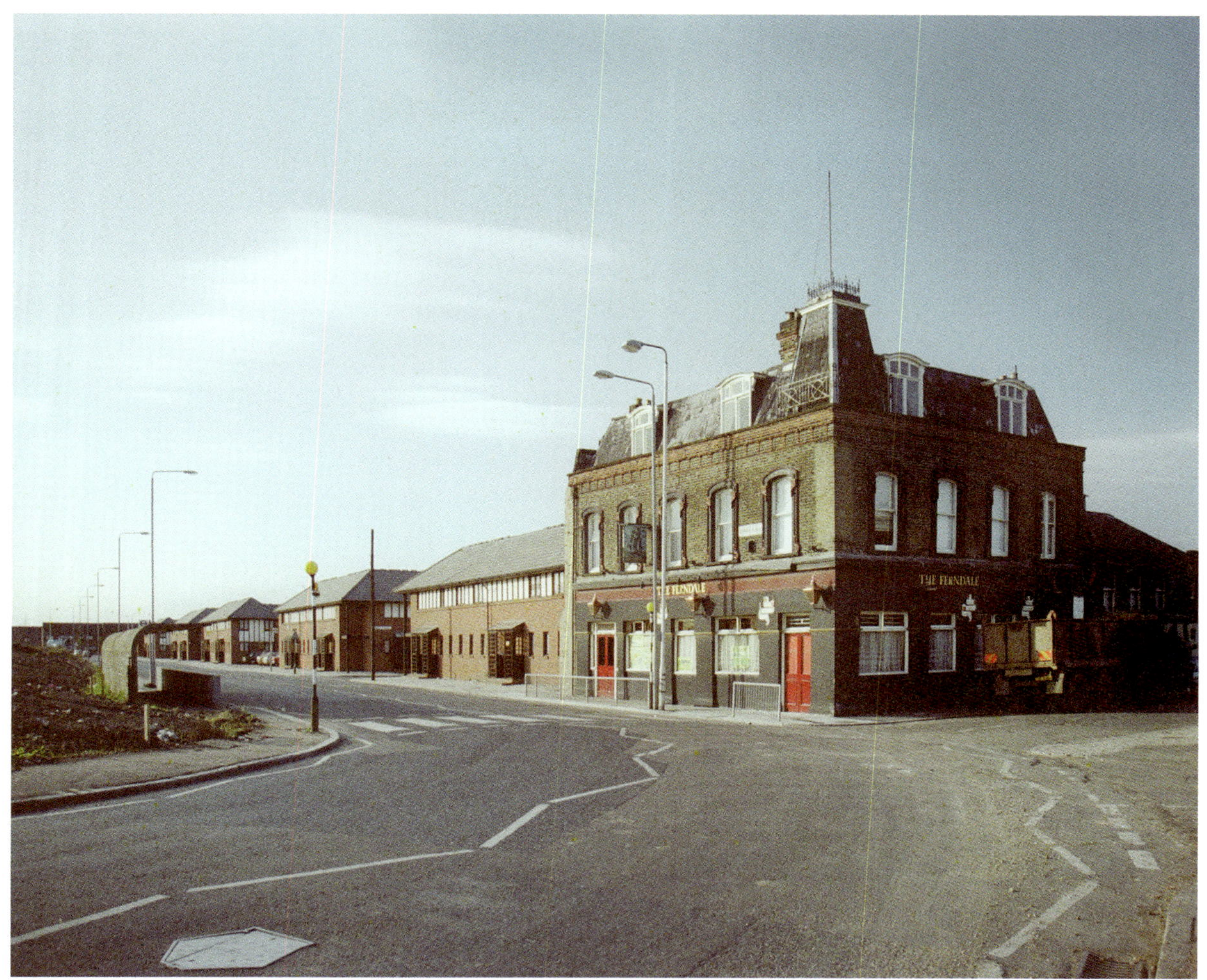

The Ferndale, Cyprus Place, 1987

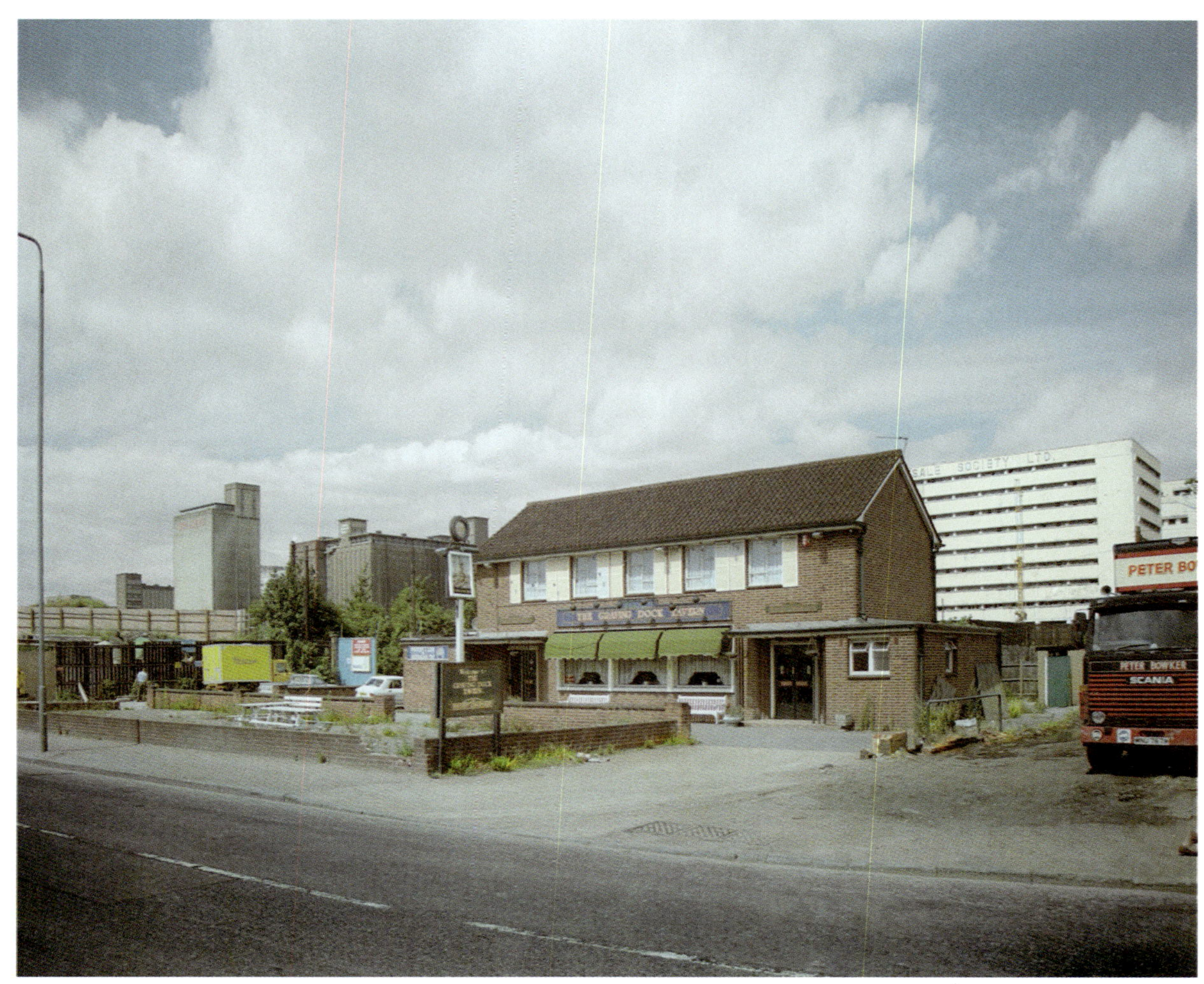

The Graving Dock Tavern, North Woolwich Road, 1987

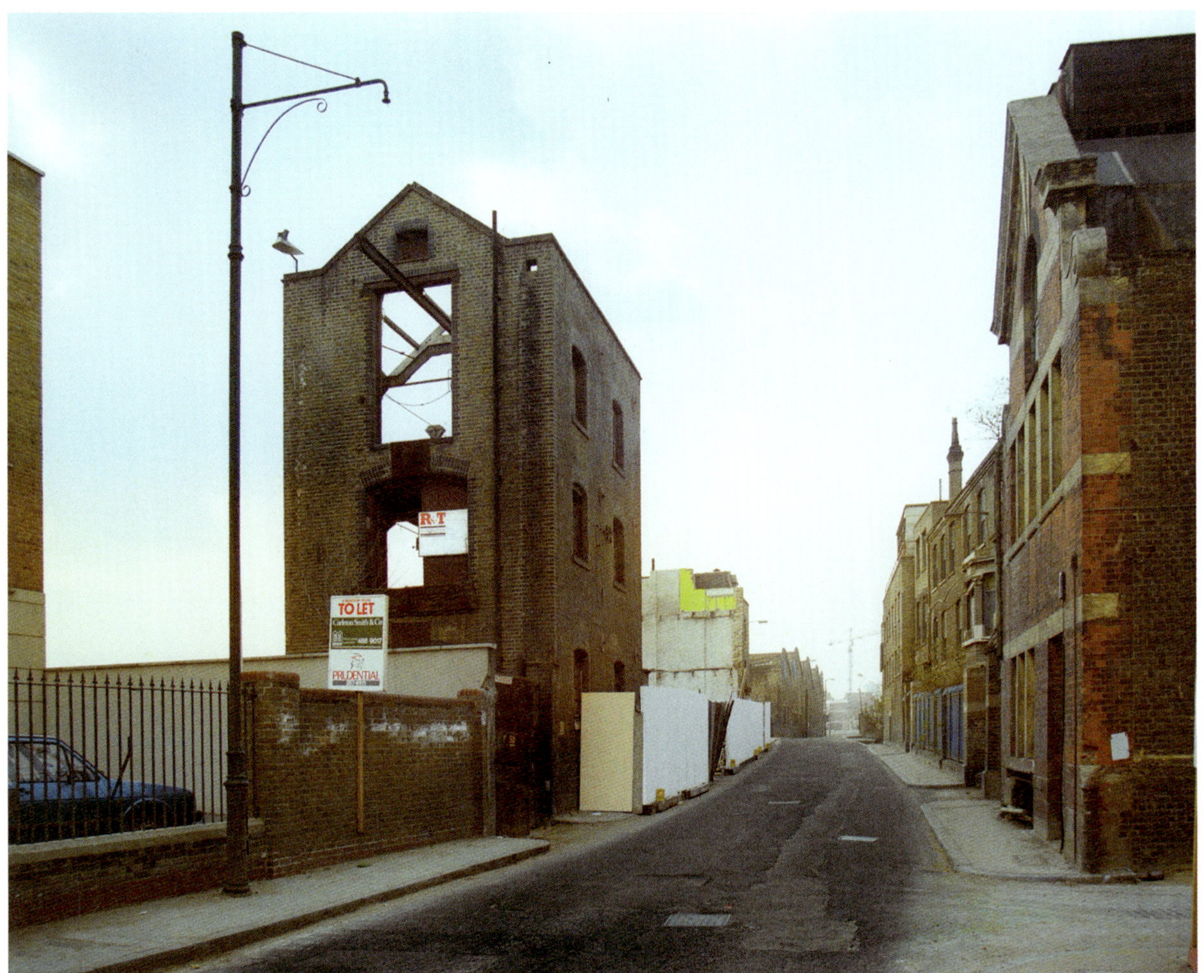

Narrow Street, 1988

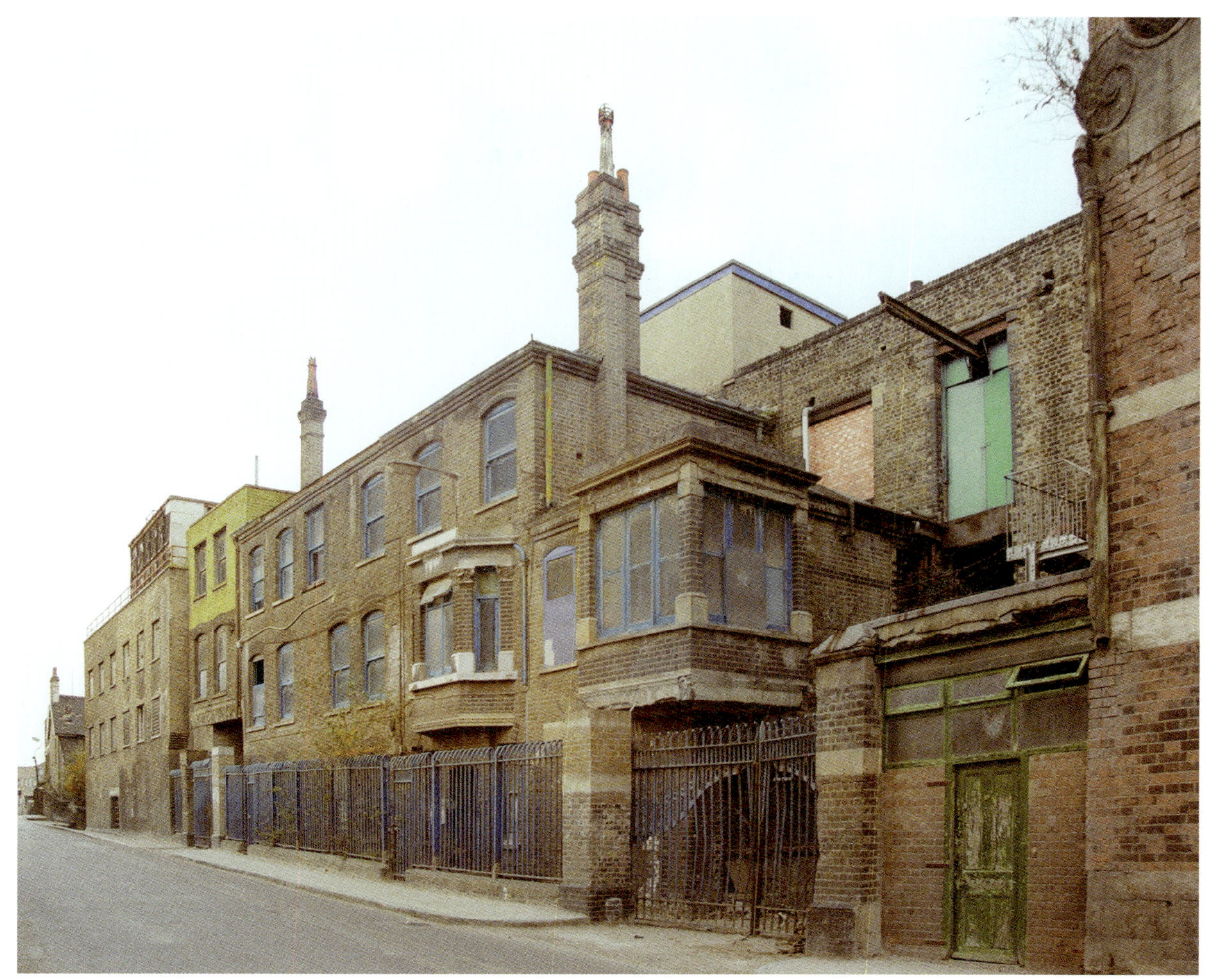

Narrow Street, 1988

Leslie's Café, Prestons Road, 1988

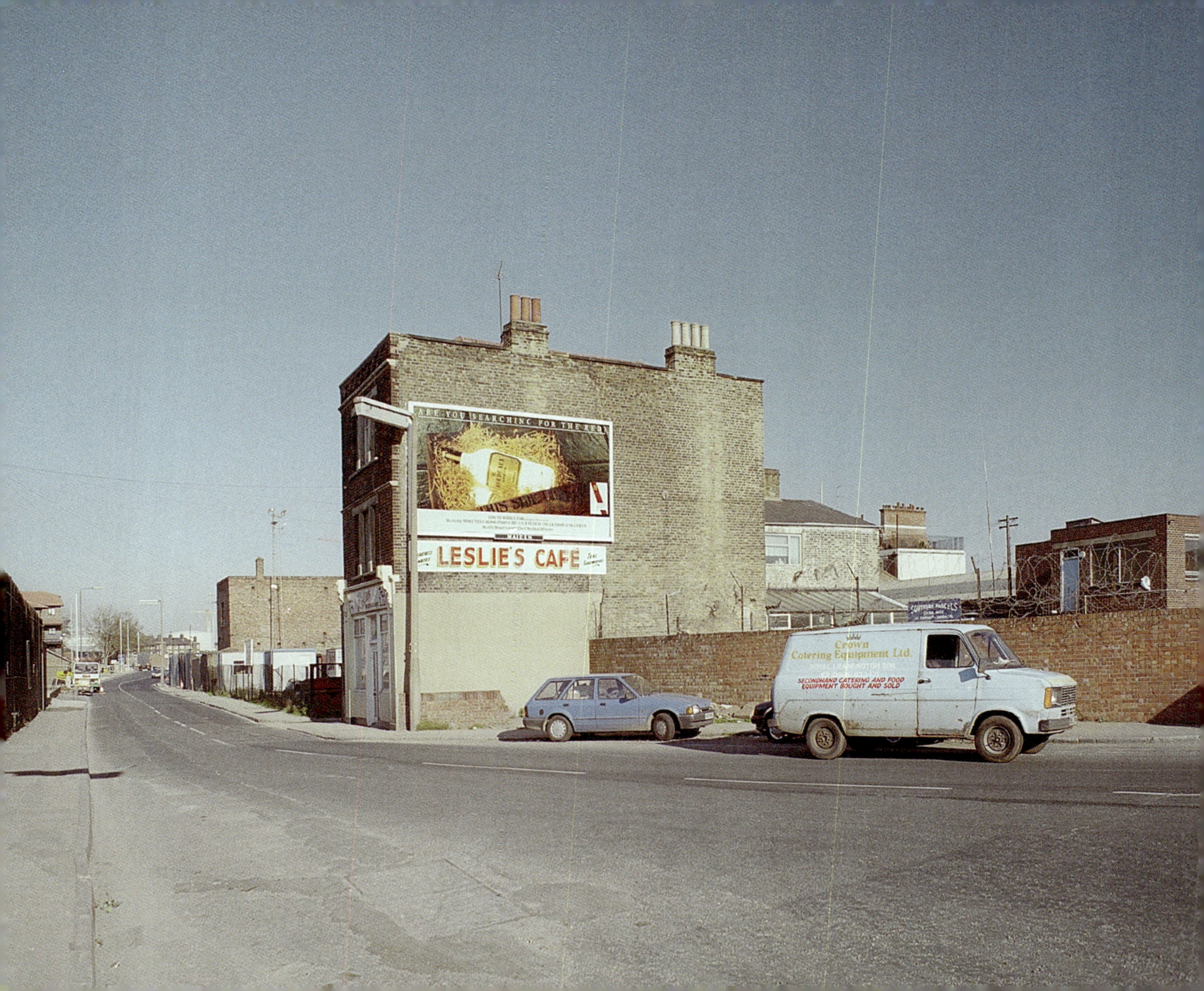
ARE YOU SEARCHING FOR THE BEST
LESLIE'S CAFE
Crown
Catering Equipment Ltd.
SECONDHAND CATERING AND FOOD
EQUIPMENT BOUGHT AND SOLD

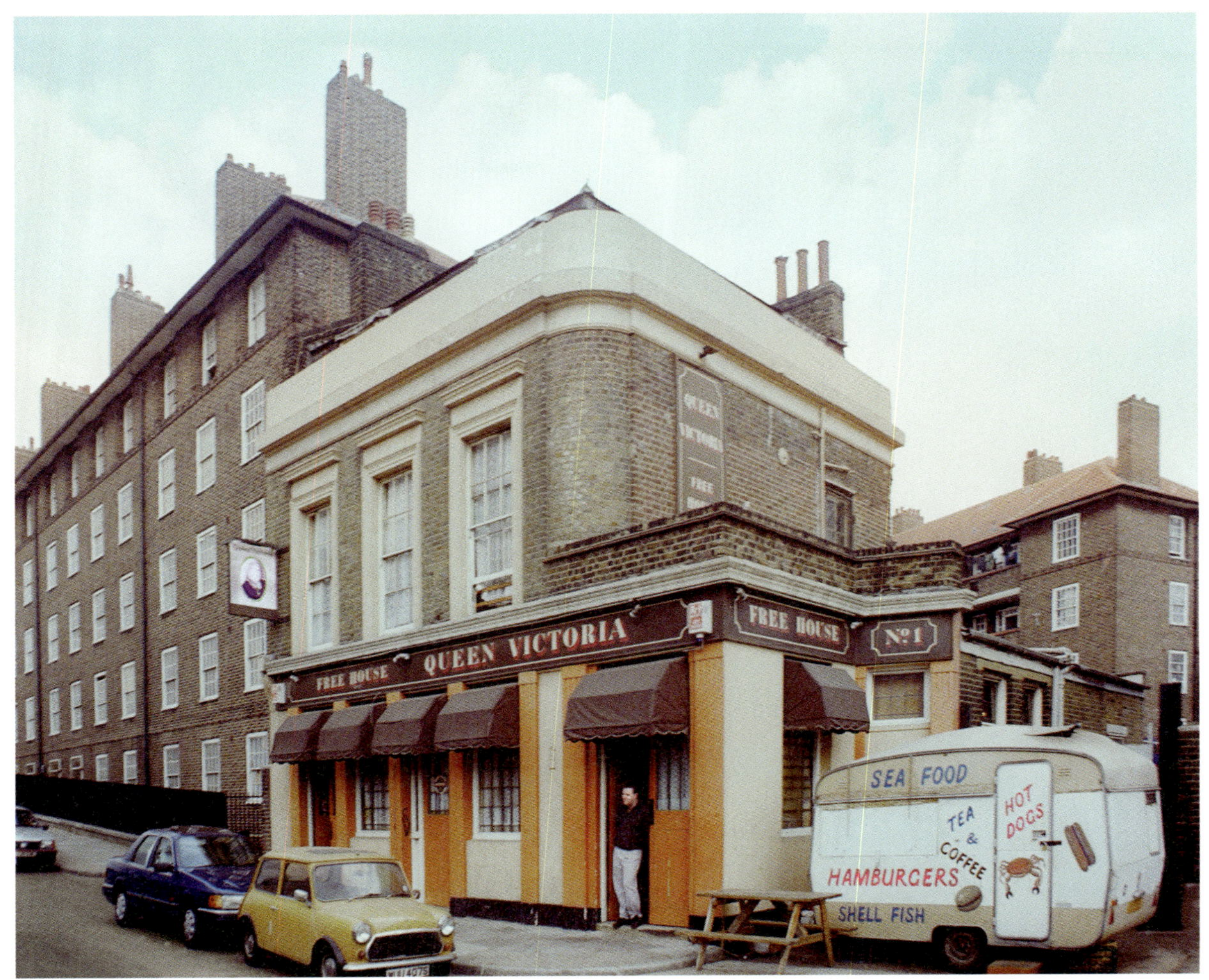

Queen Victoria, Gillender Street, 1990

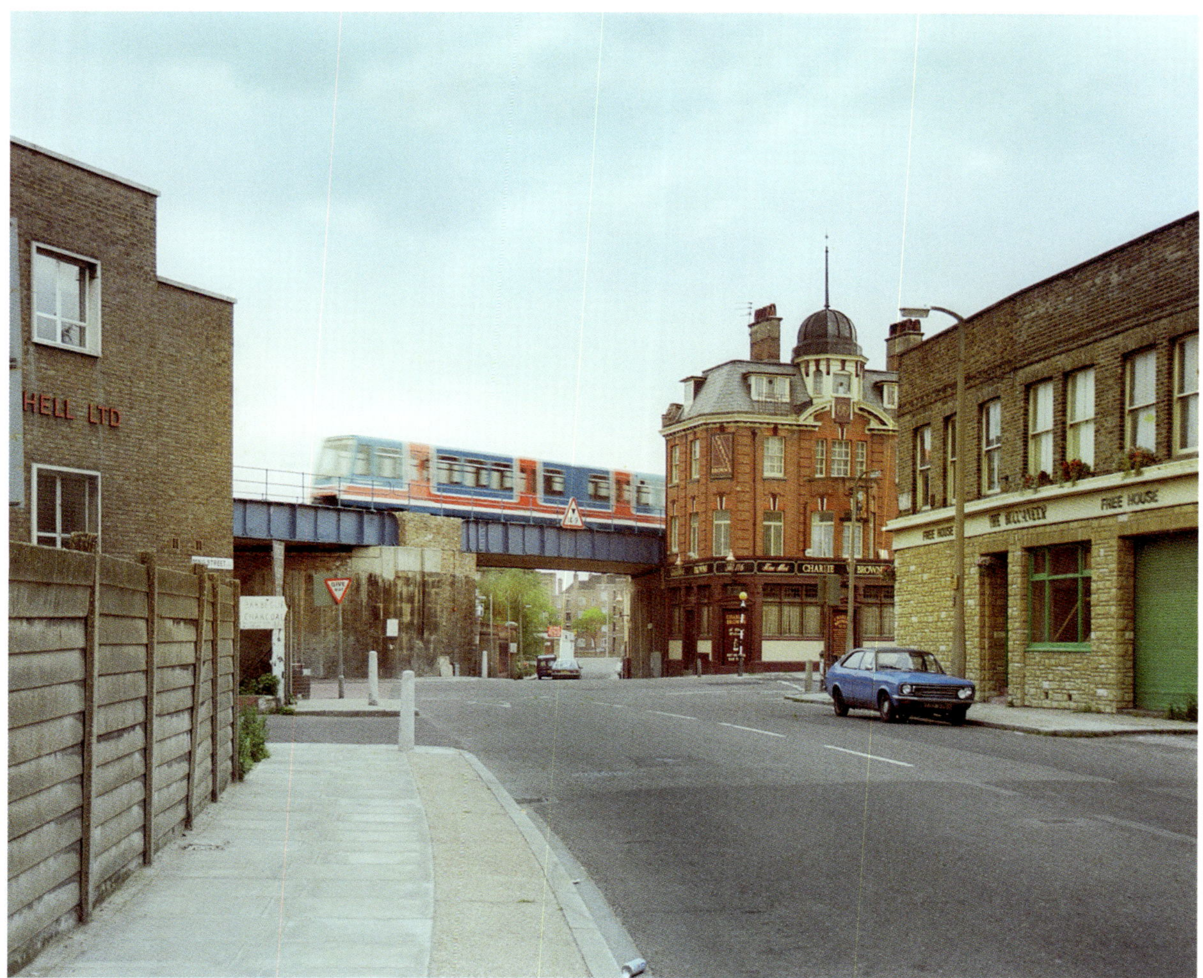

Ming Street, 1987

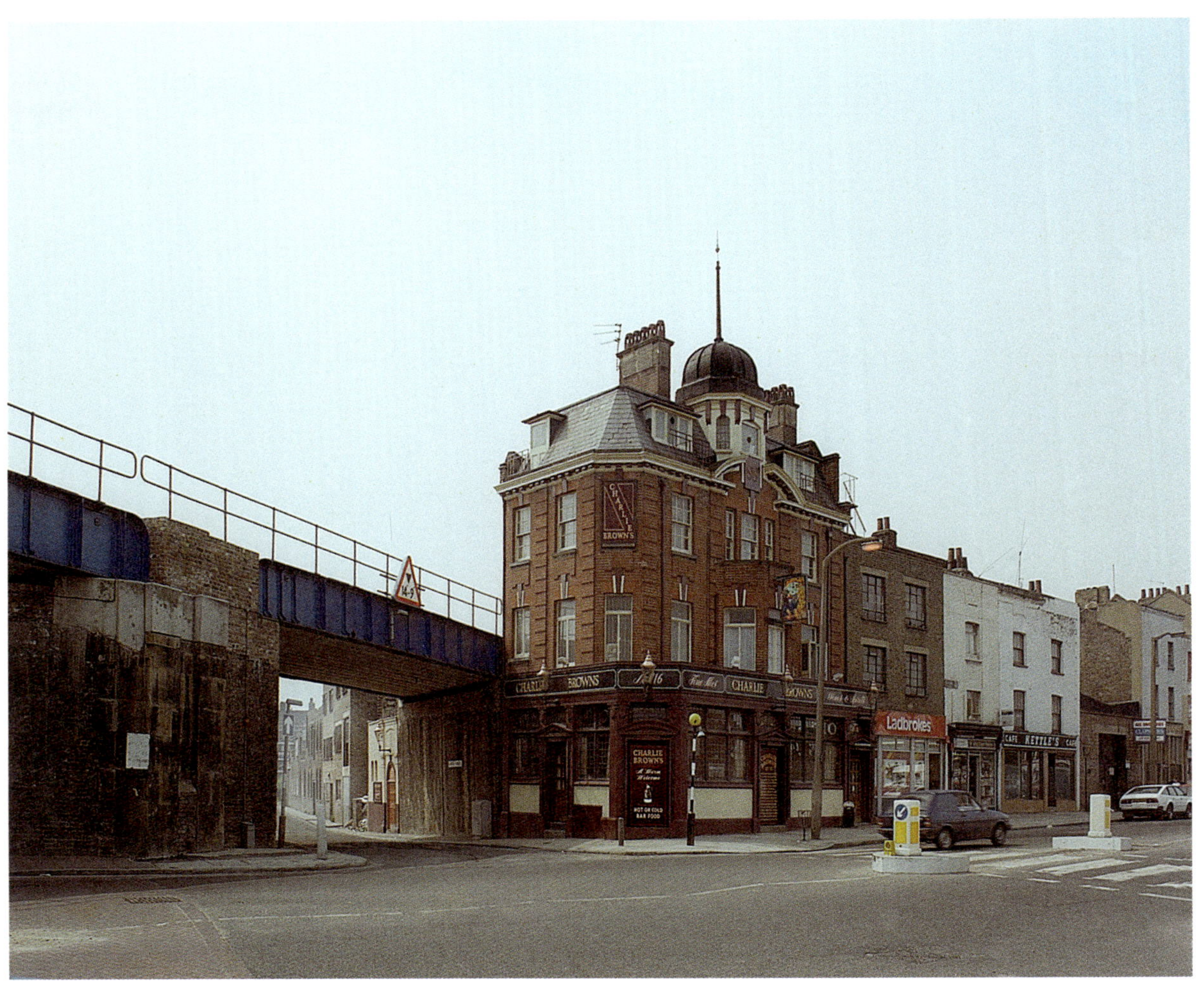

Charlie Brown's, West India Dock Road, 1988

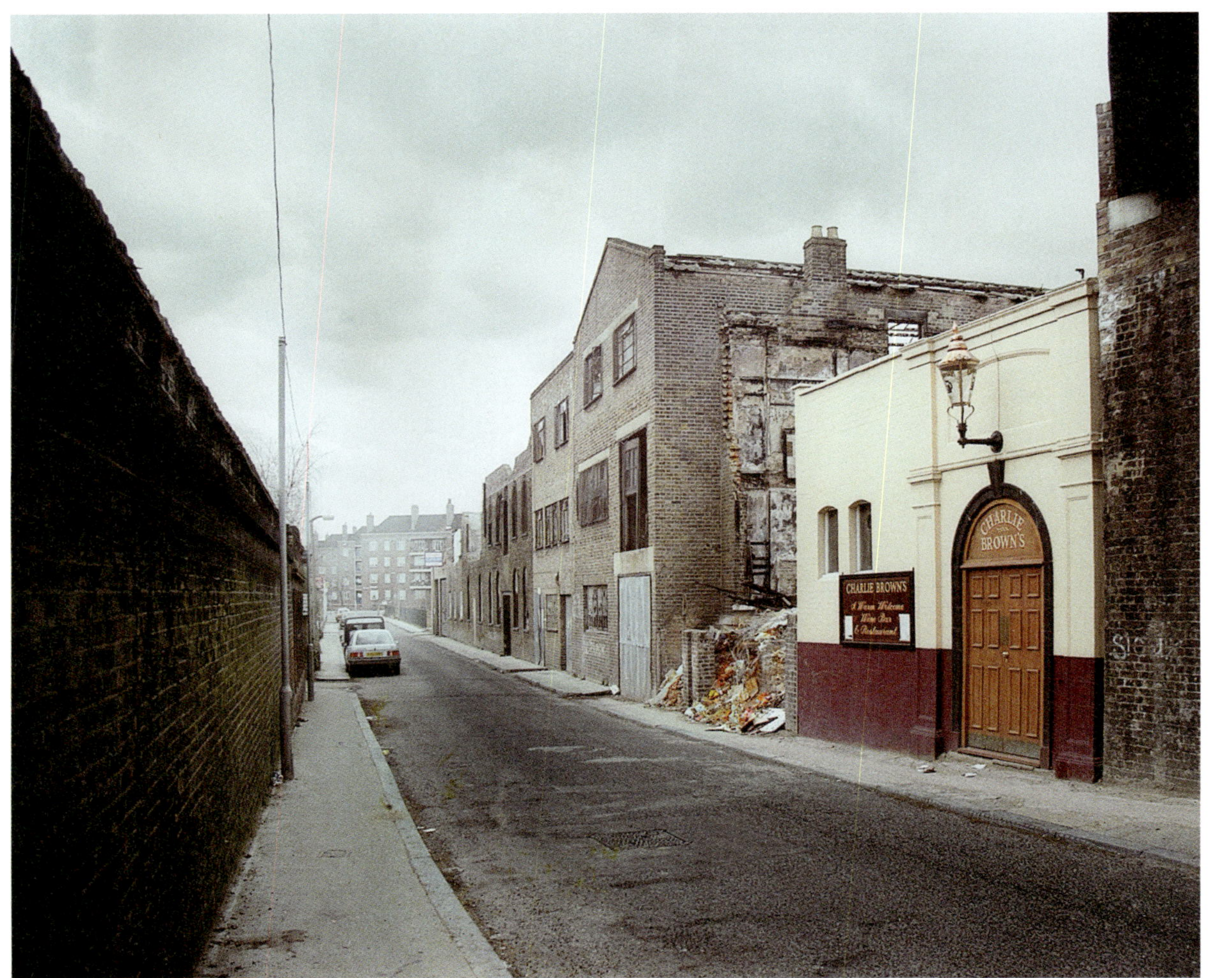

Garford Street, 1988

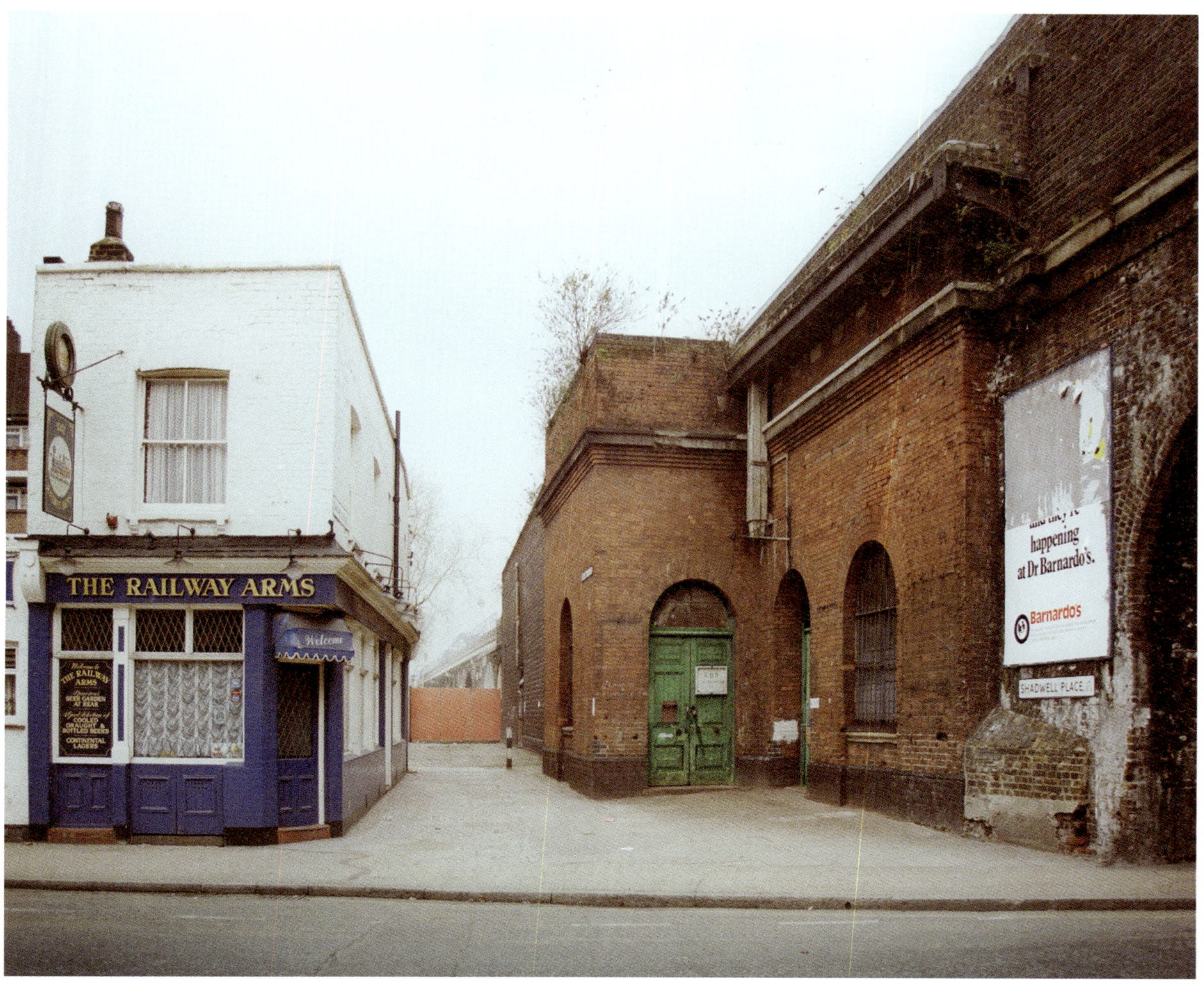

The Railway Arms, Shadwell Place, 1987

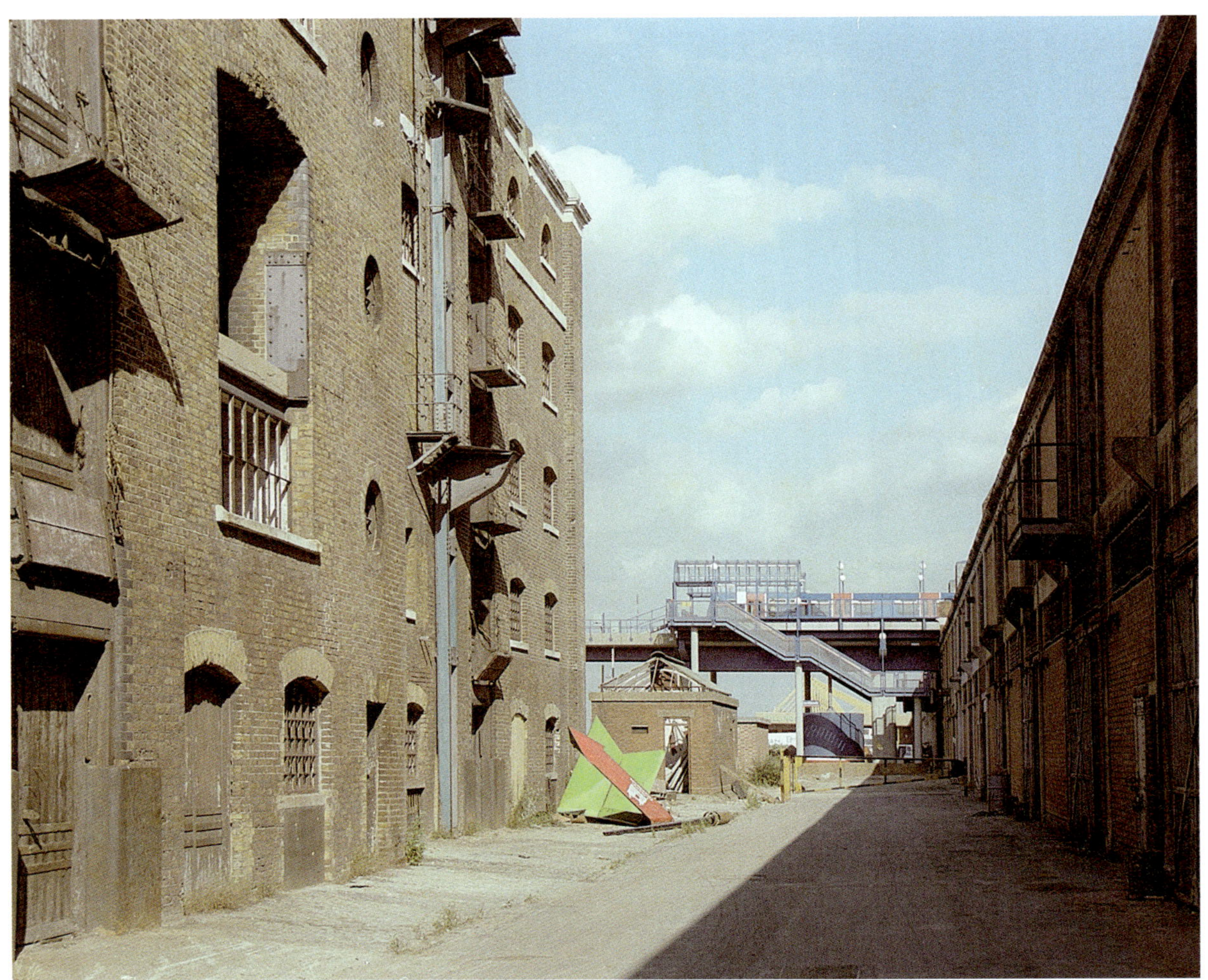

West India Quay DLR station, 1987

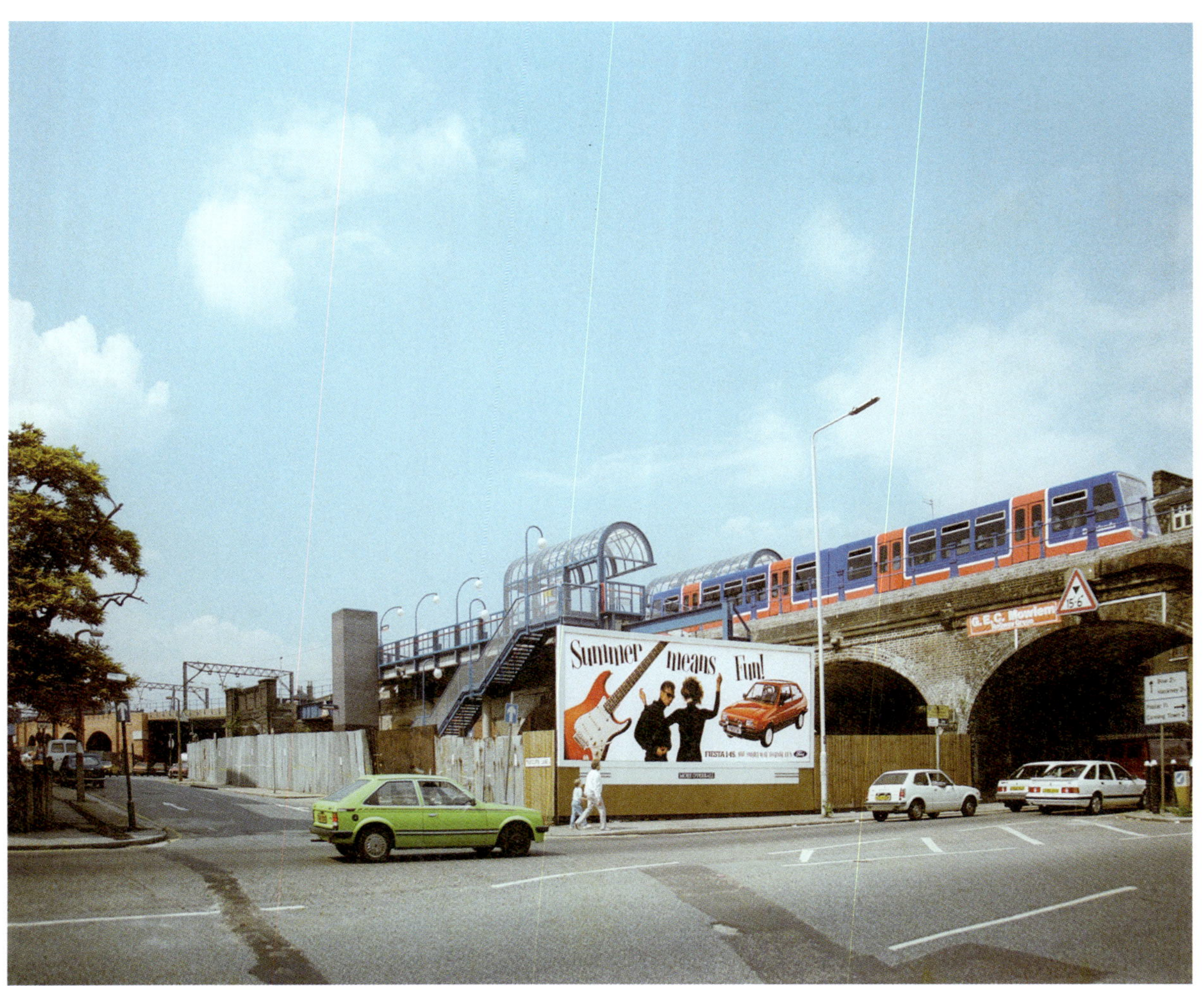

Limehouse DLR station, Branch Road, 1987

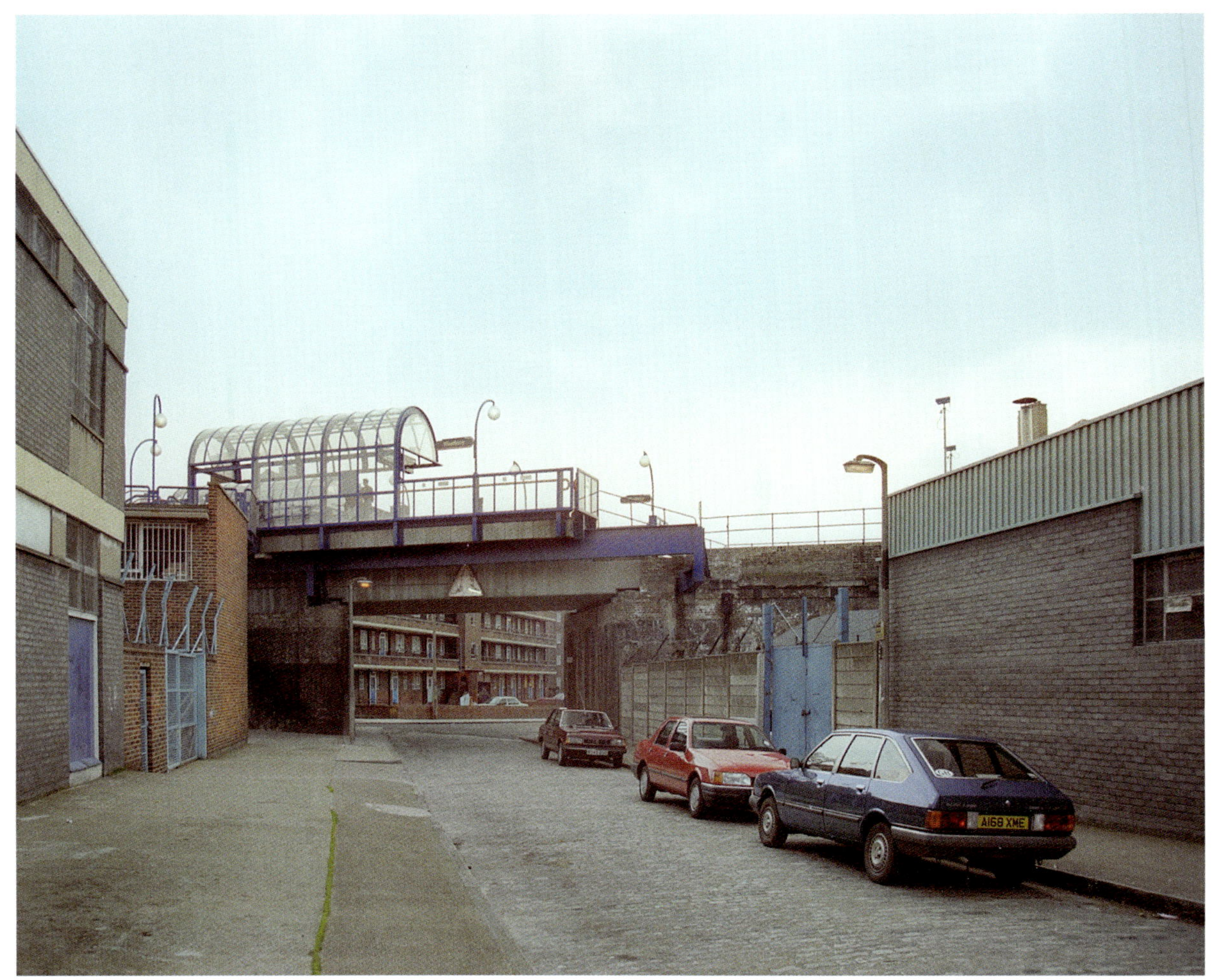
Westferry DLR station, Salter Street, 1988

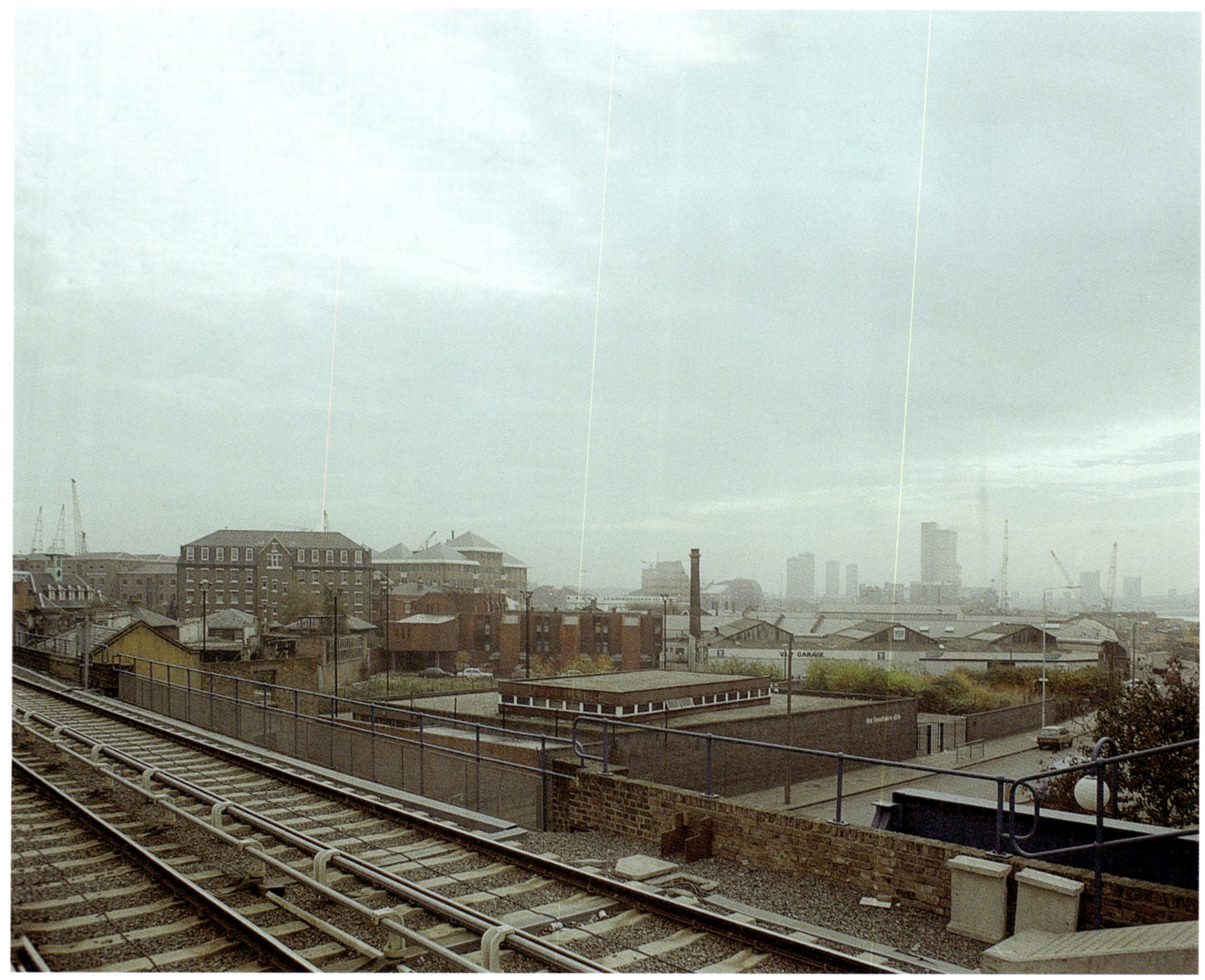

View from Westferry DLR station, 1988

View of the City of London from Bishopsgate Goods Yard, 1981

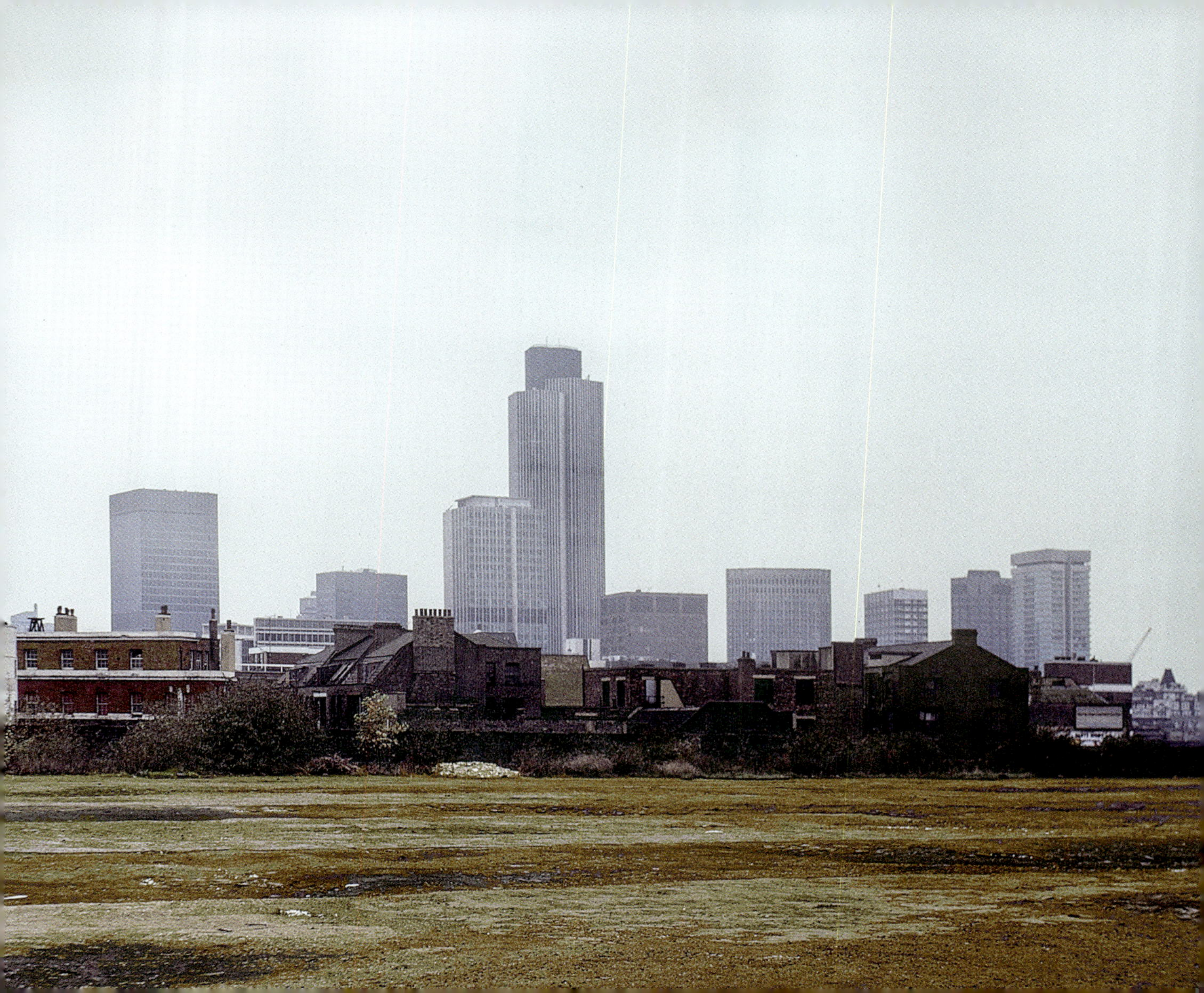

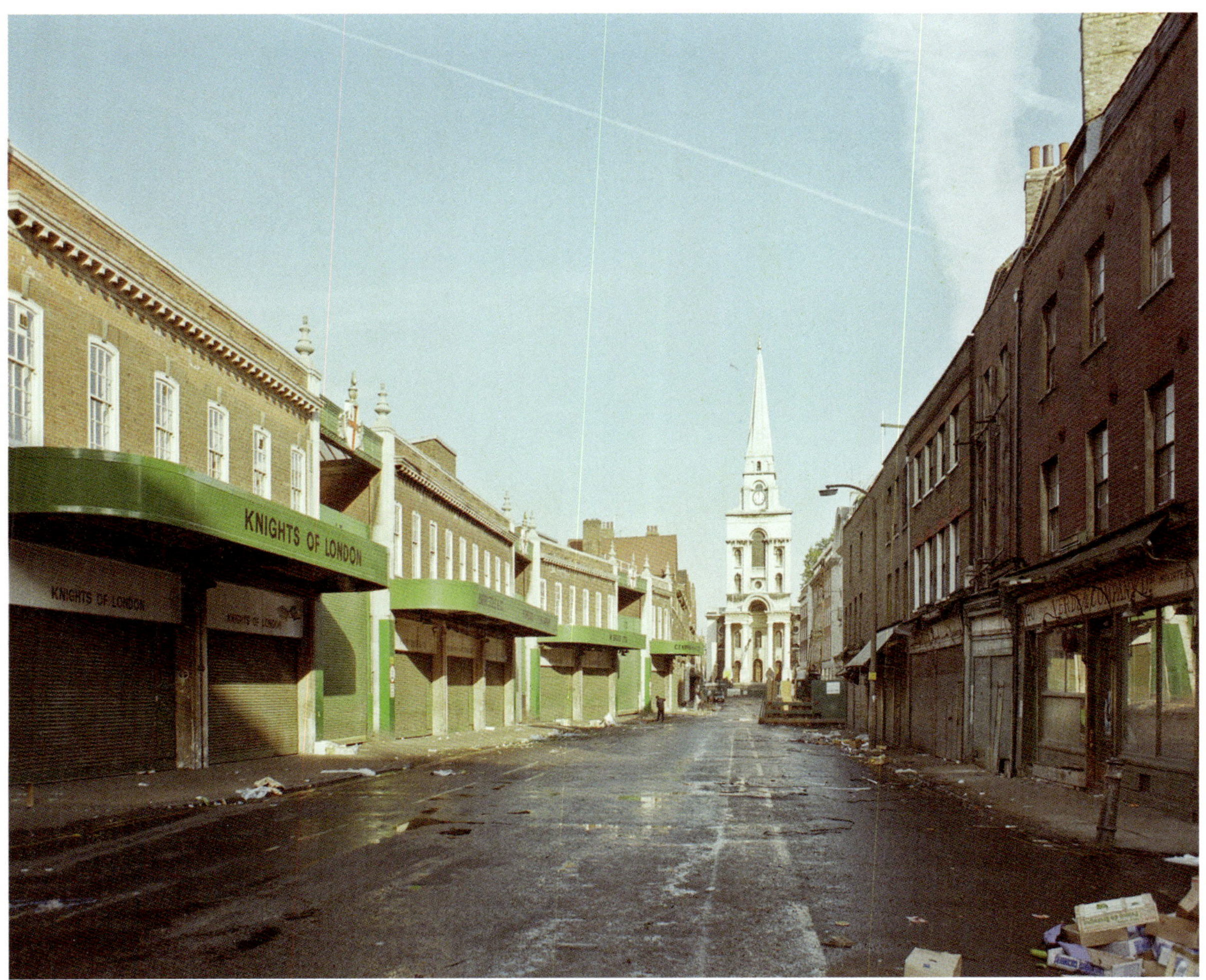

Spitalfields Market, Brushfield Street, 1988

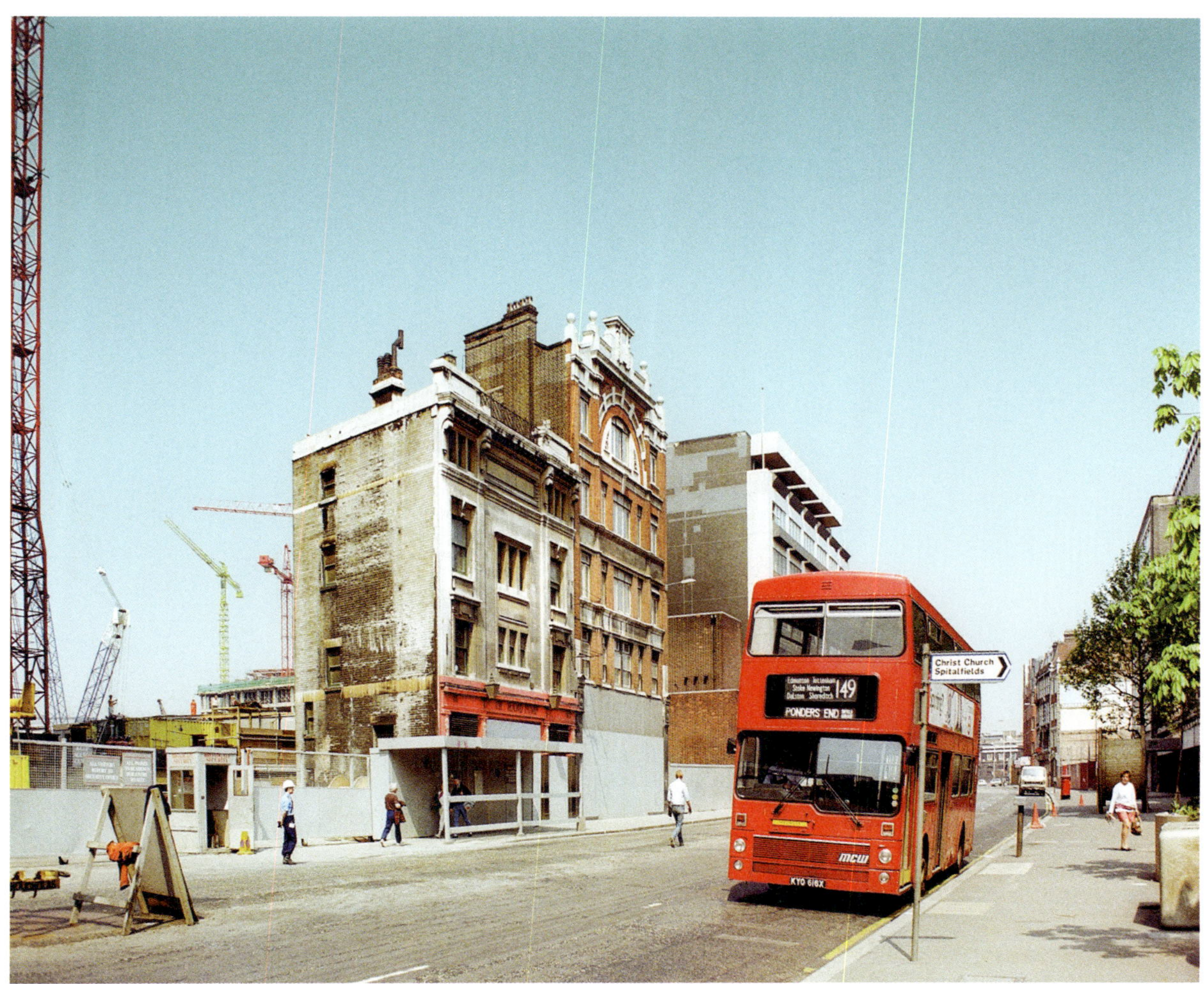

Bishopsgate, 1988

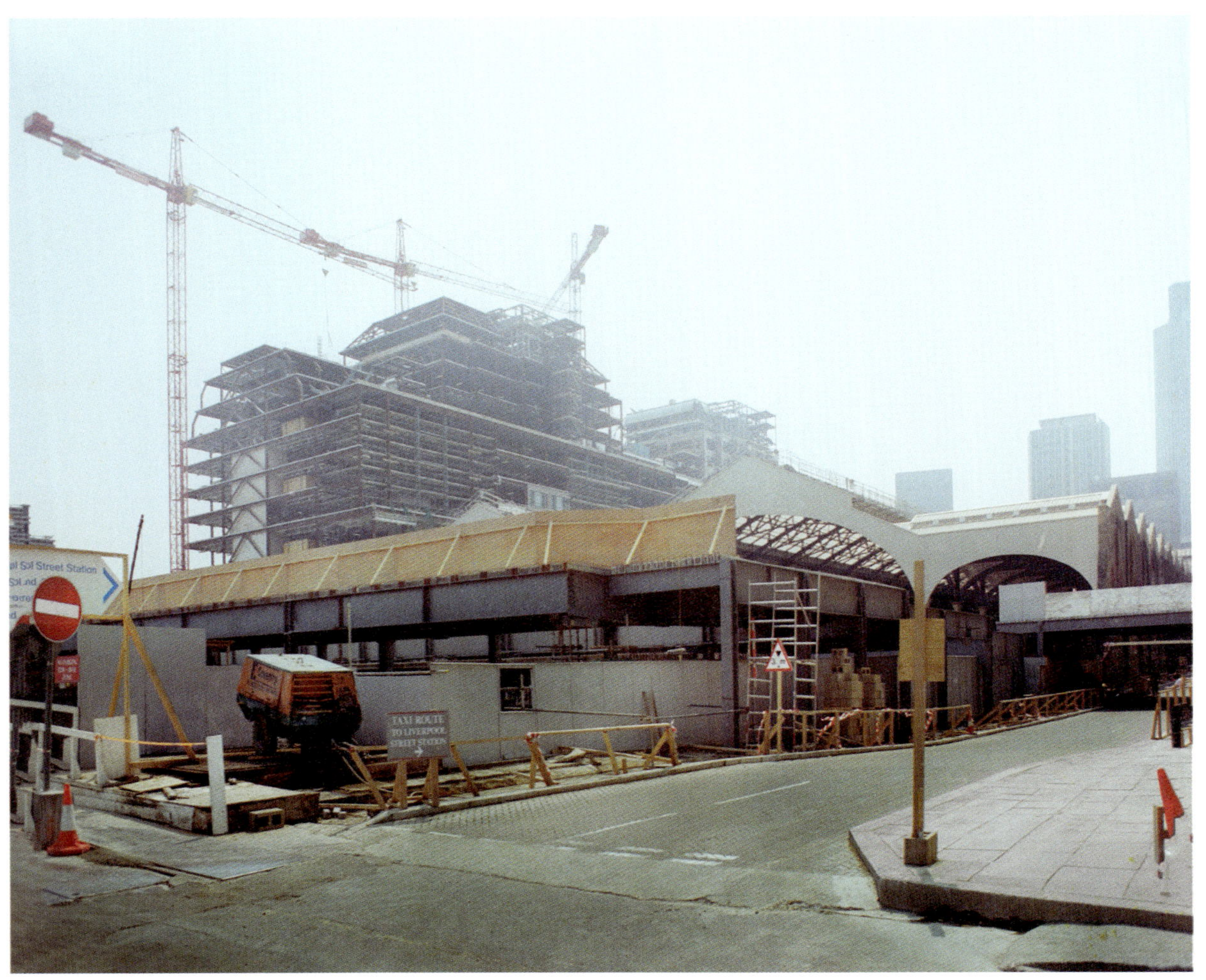

Liverpool Street station site, Pindar Street, 1988

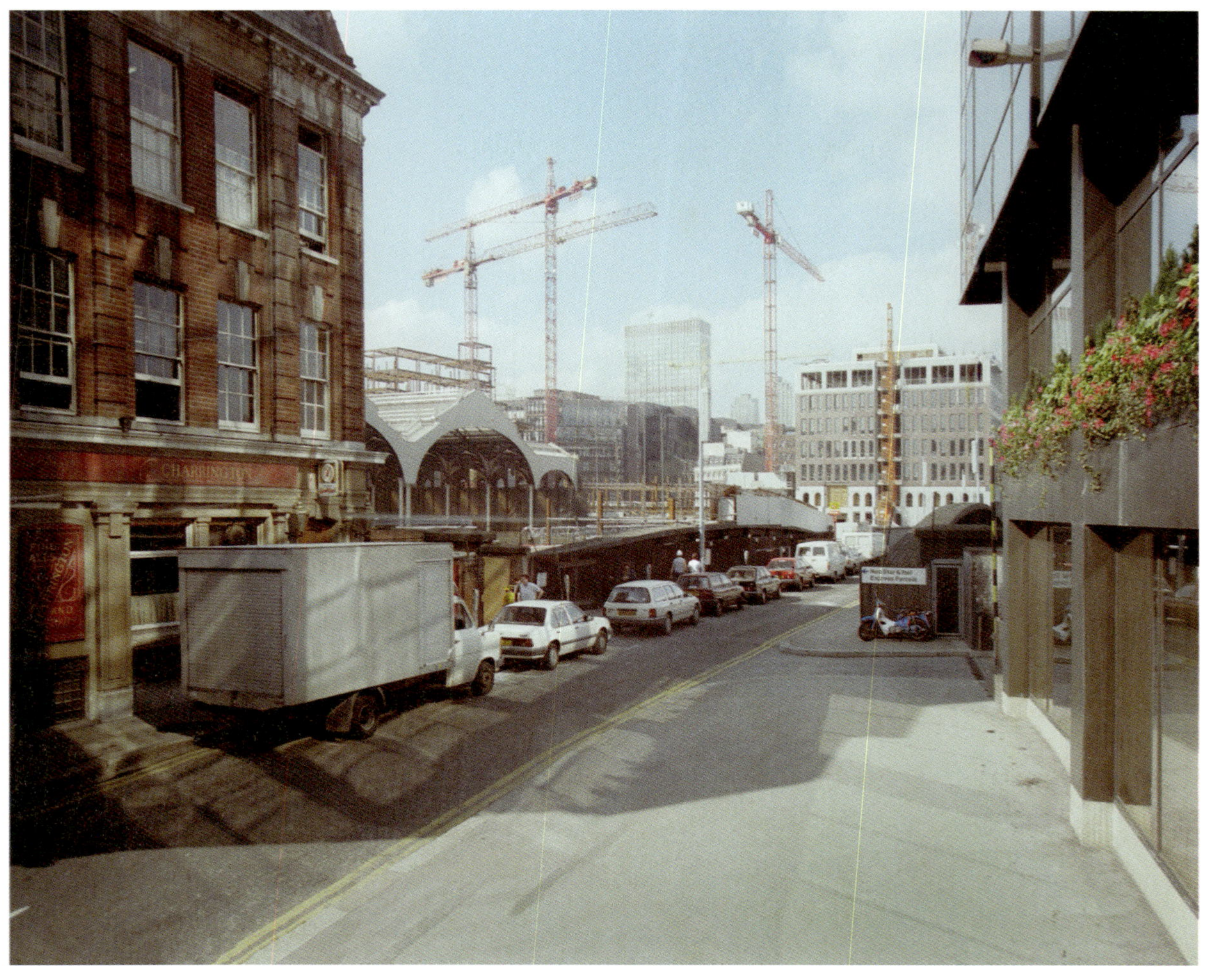

Pindar Street, 1987

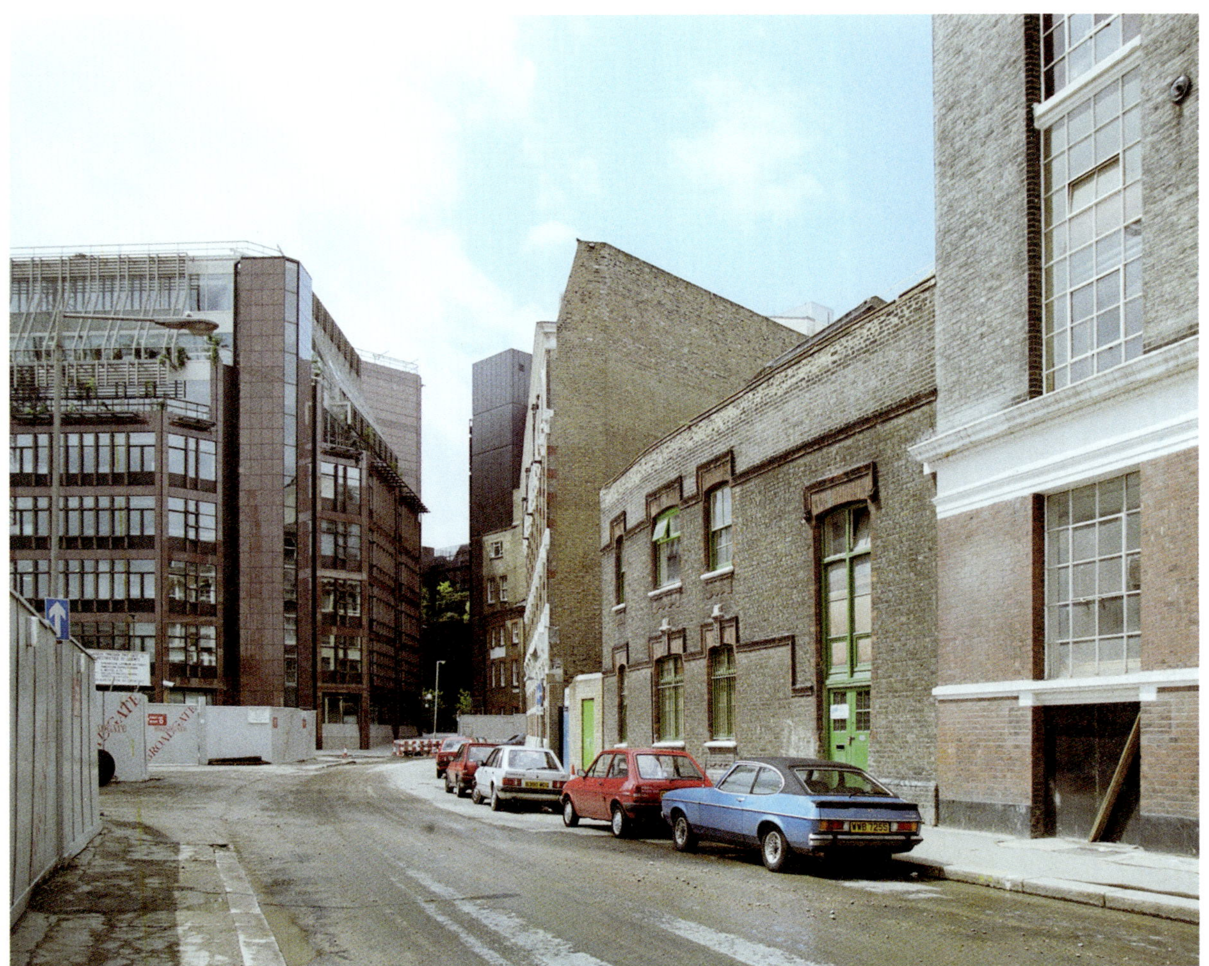

Appold Street, 1987

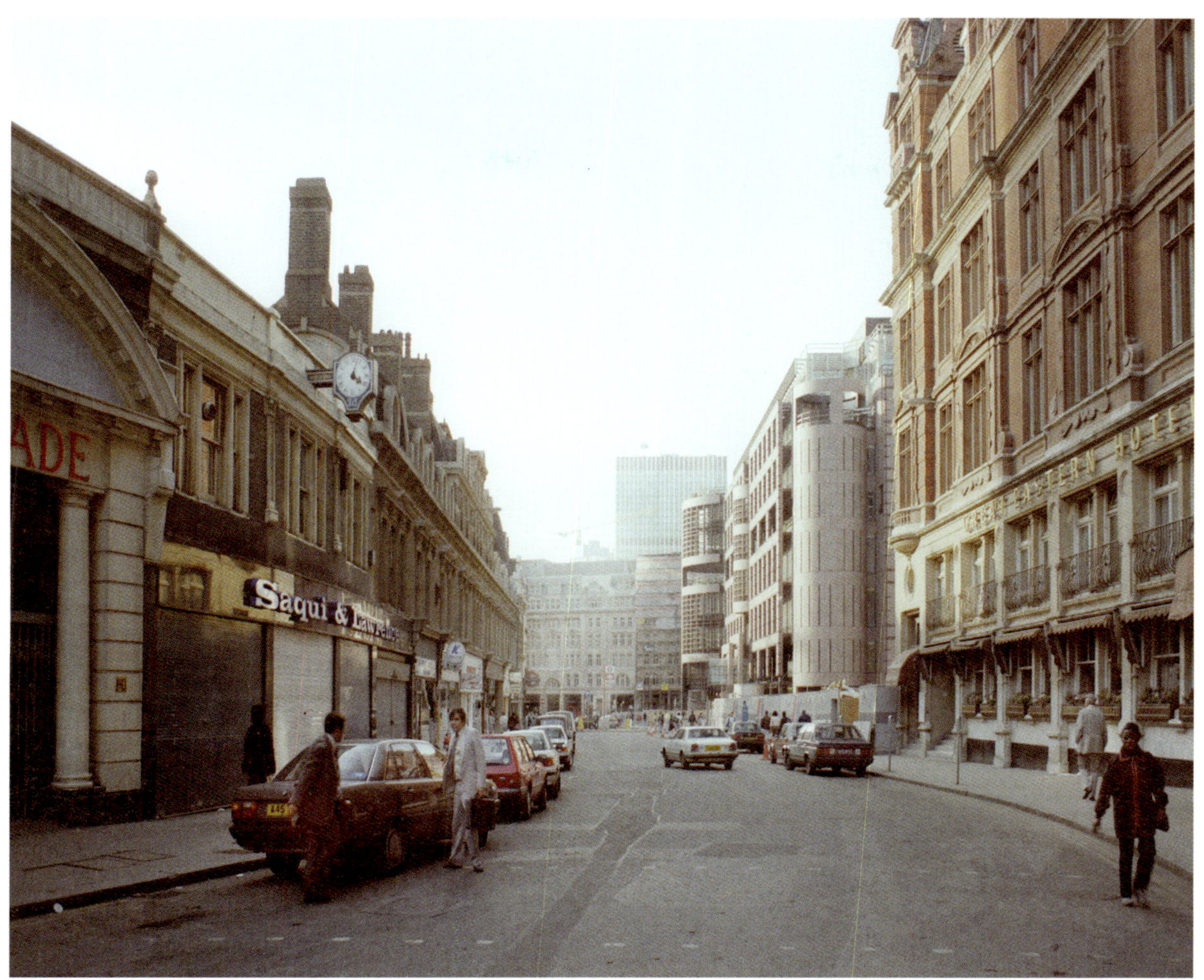

Liverpool Street, 1988

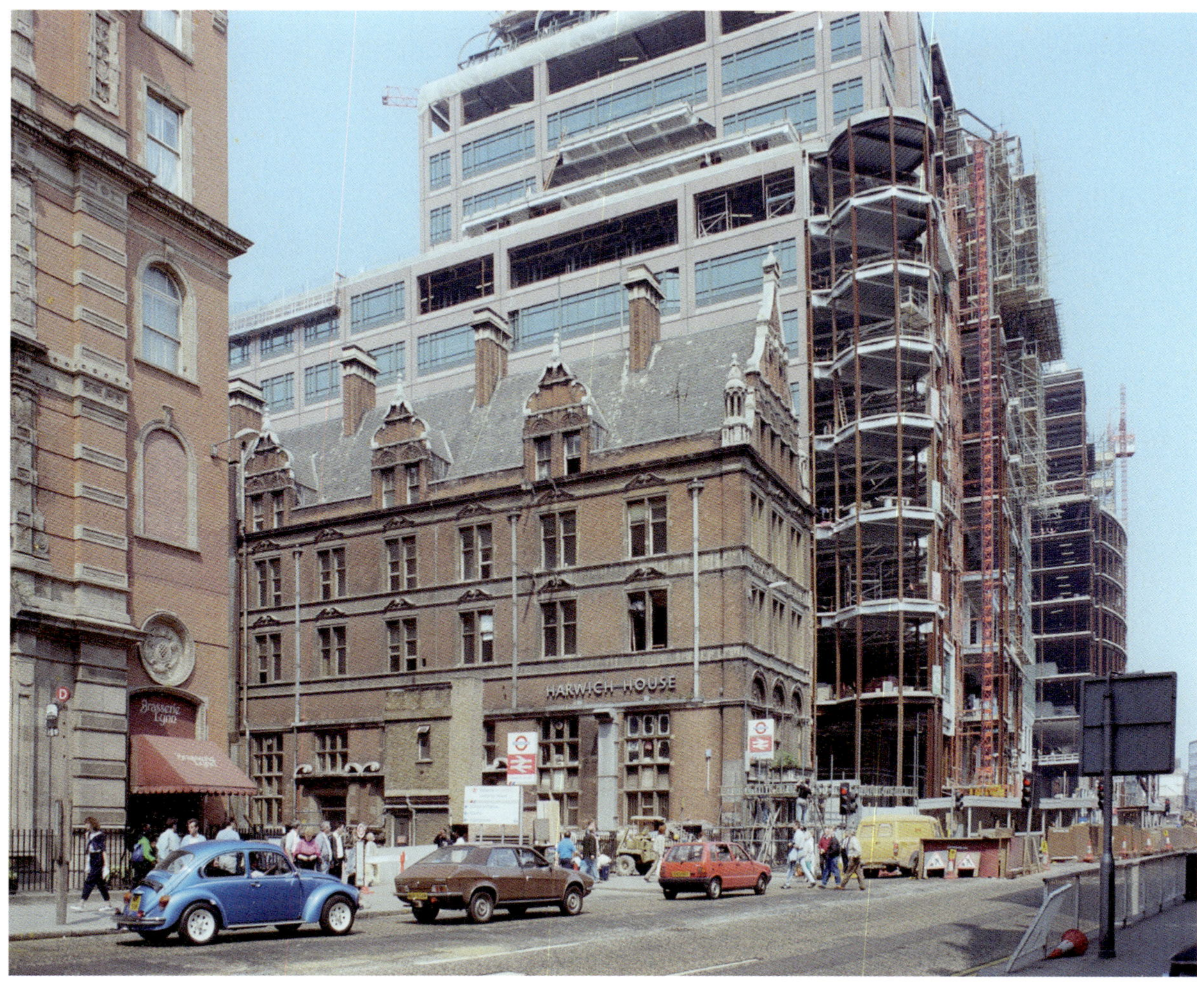

Bishopsgate, 1988

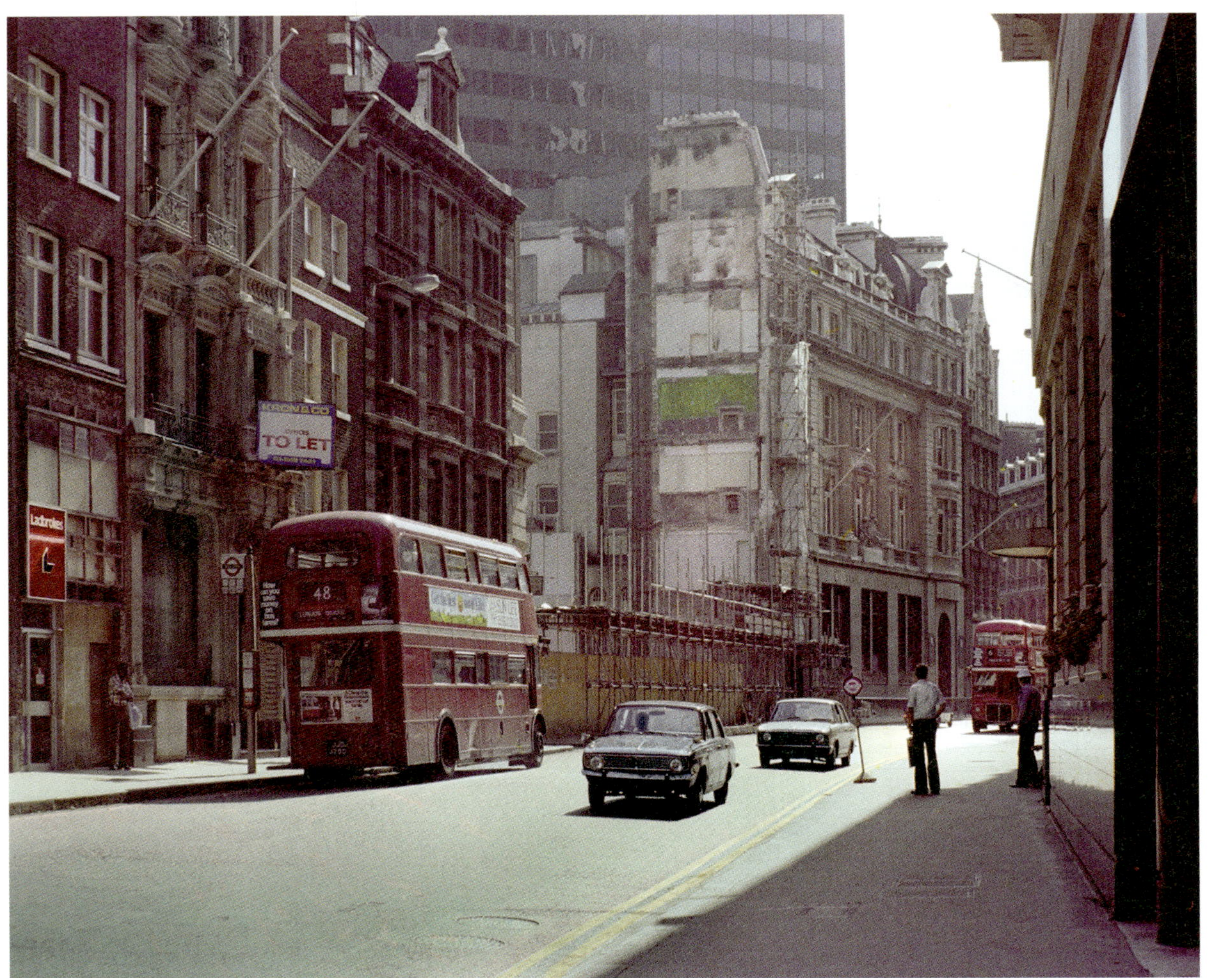

Bishopsgate, 1980

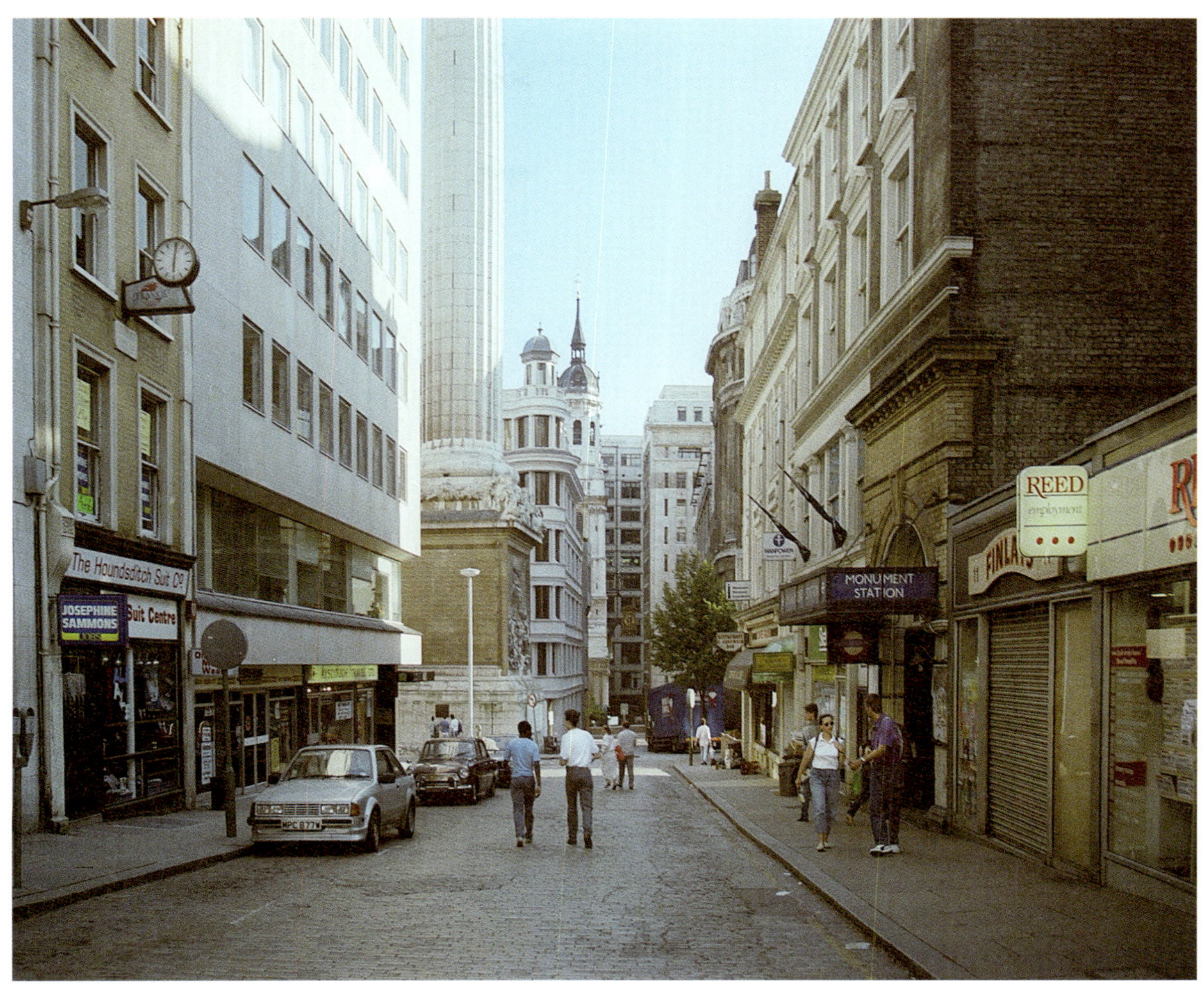

Monument Underground station, Fish Hill Street, 1987

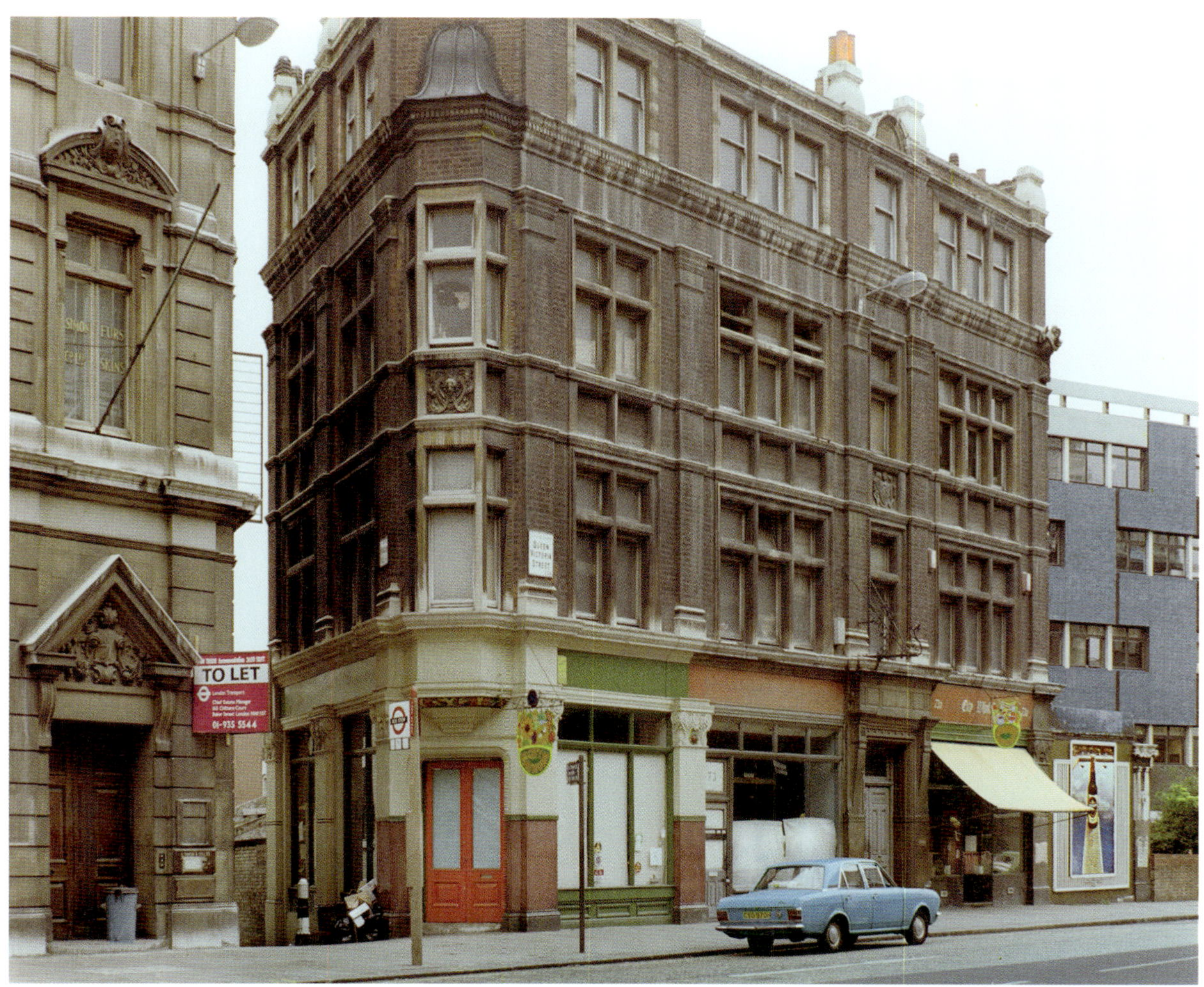

Queen Victoria Street, 1980

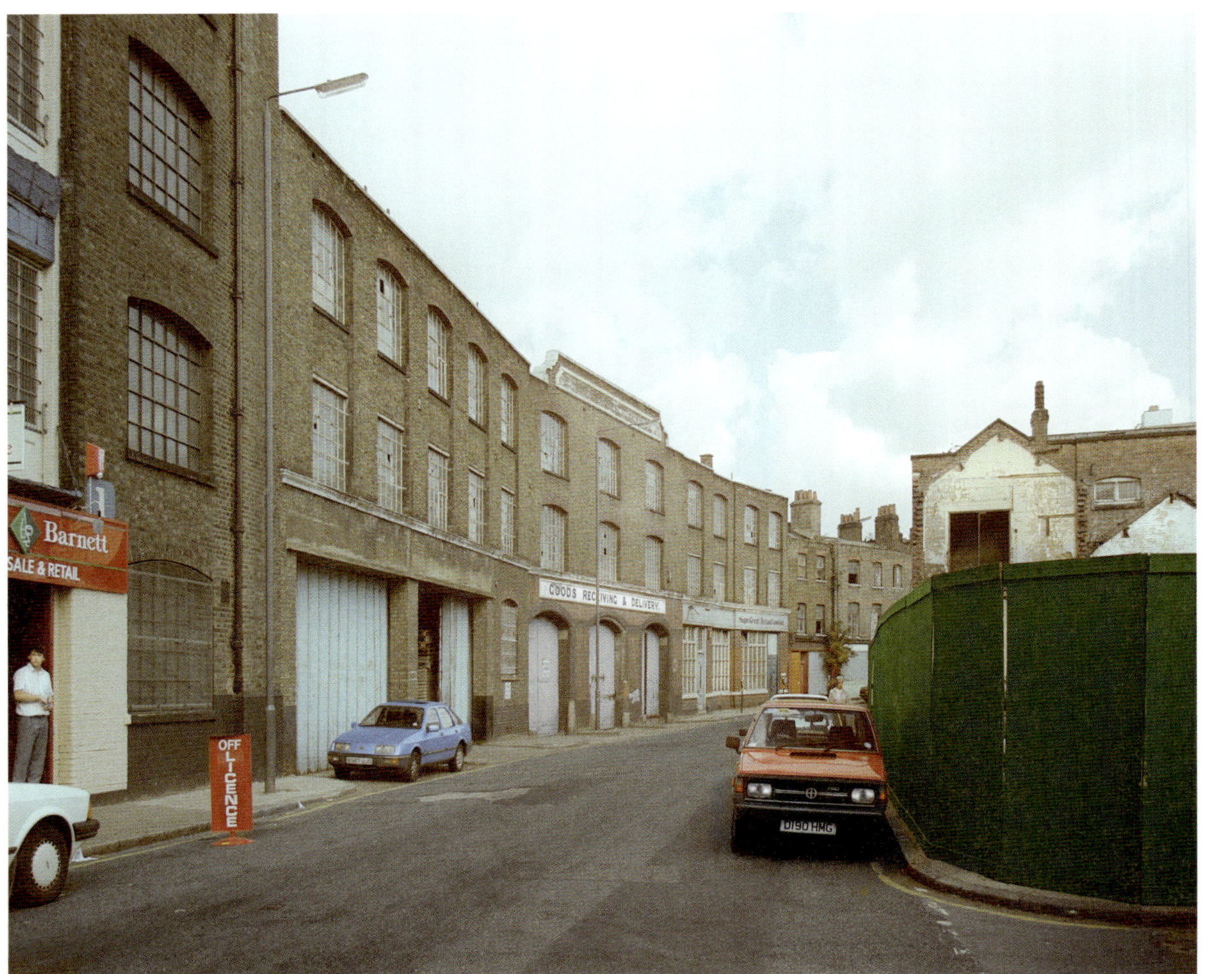

Back Church Lane, 1987

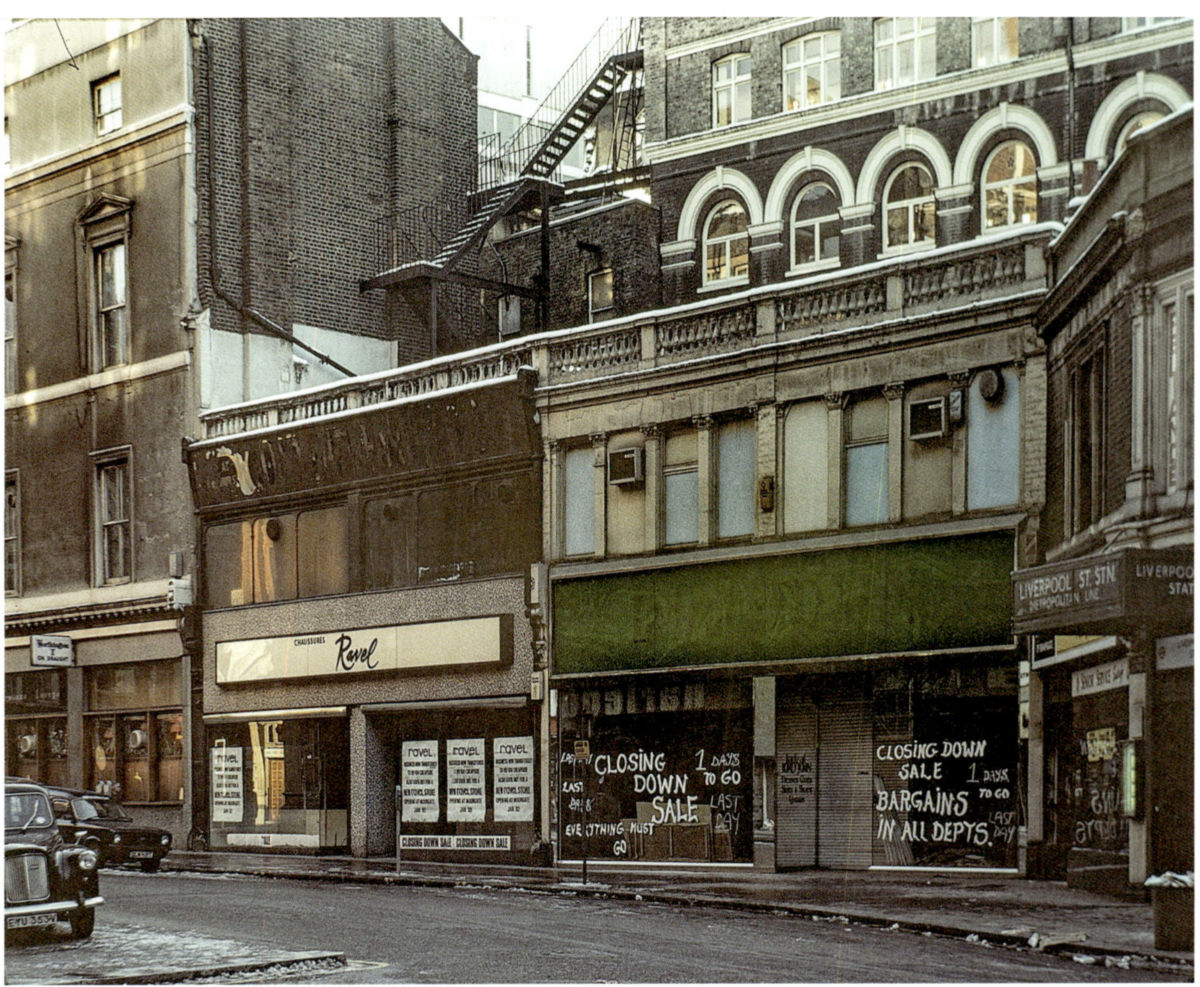

Liverpool Street, 1981

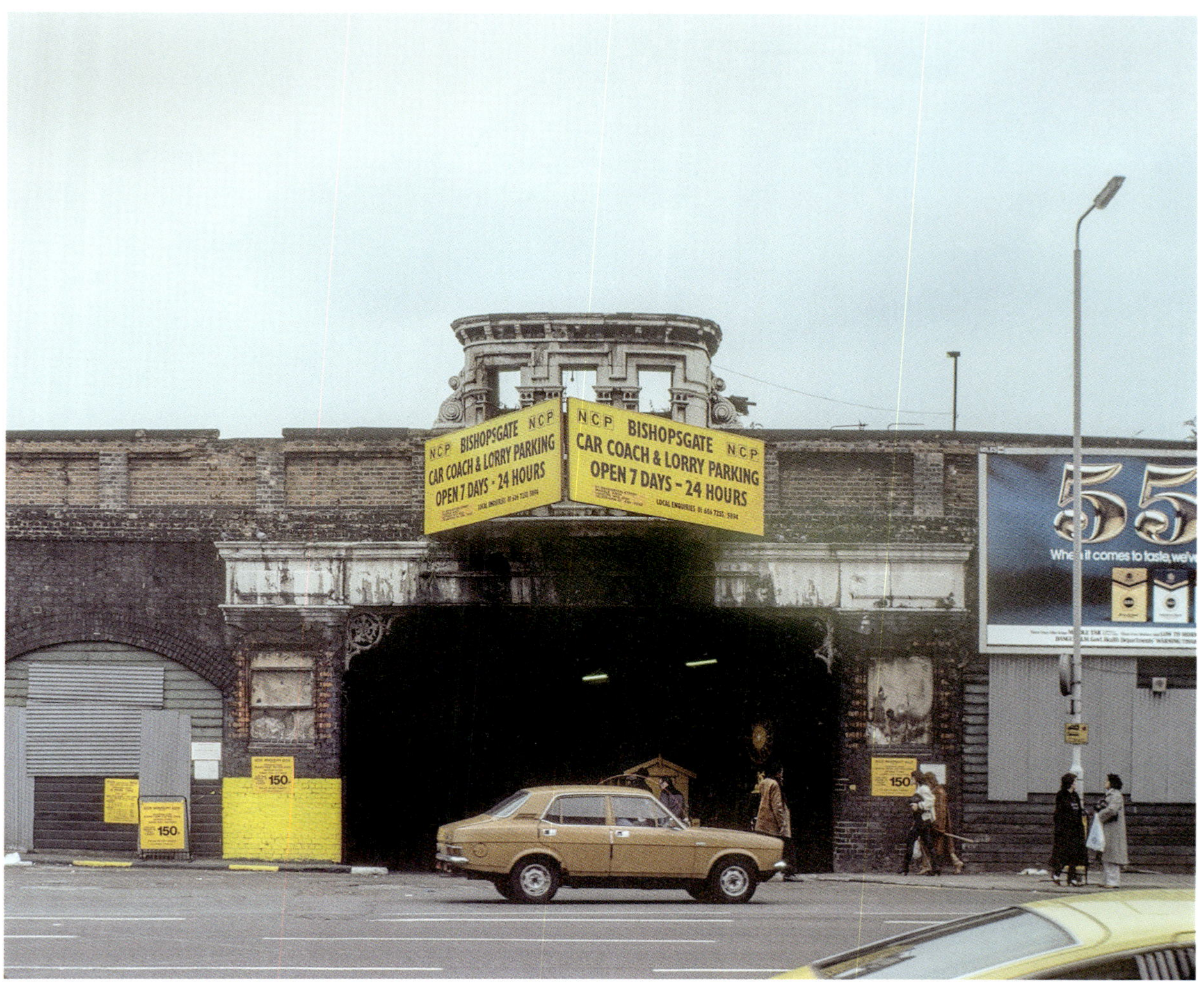

Bishopsgate Goods Yard, 1981

Stoney Street, 1981

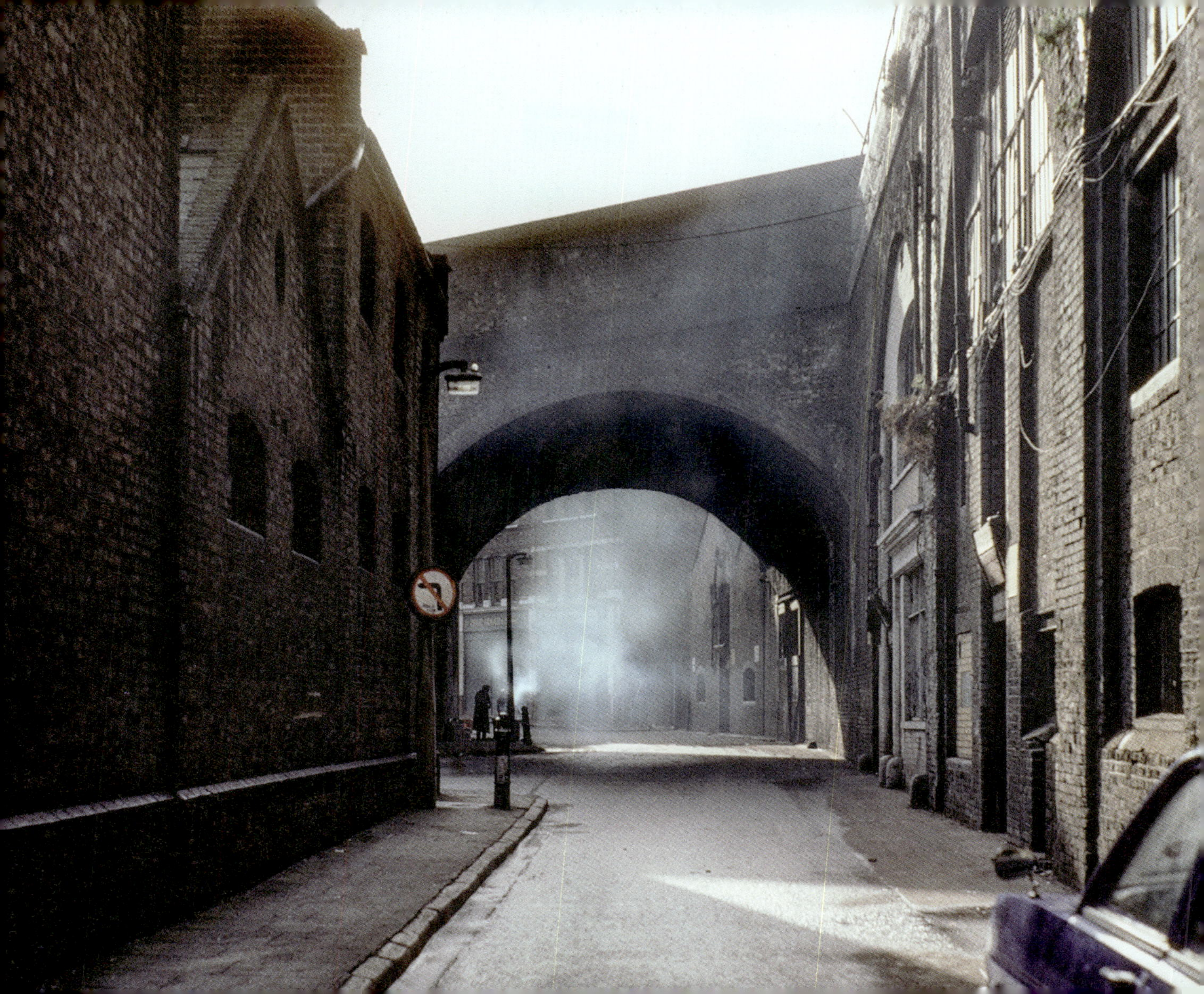

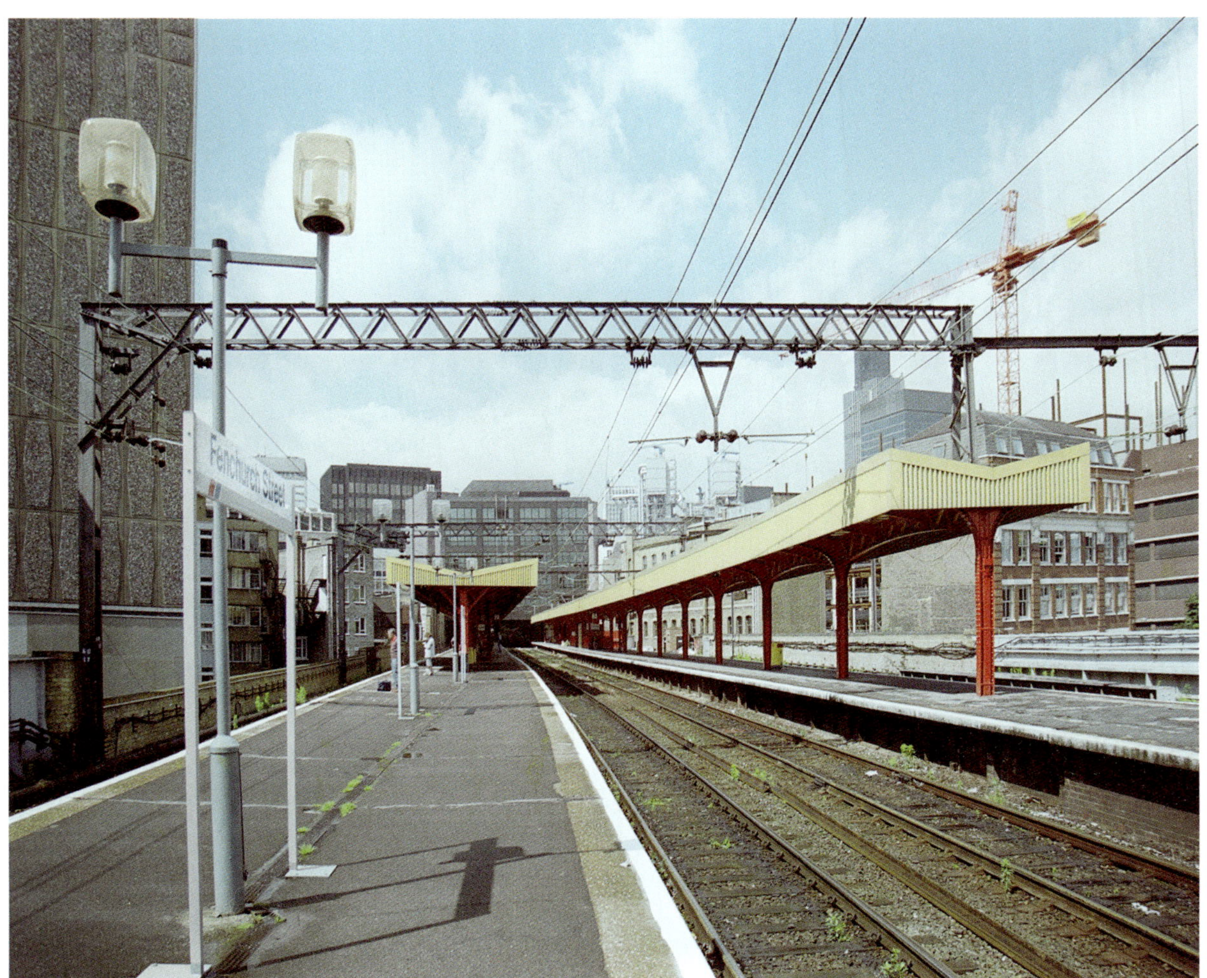

Fenchurch Street station, 1987

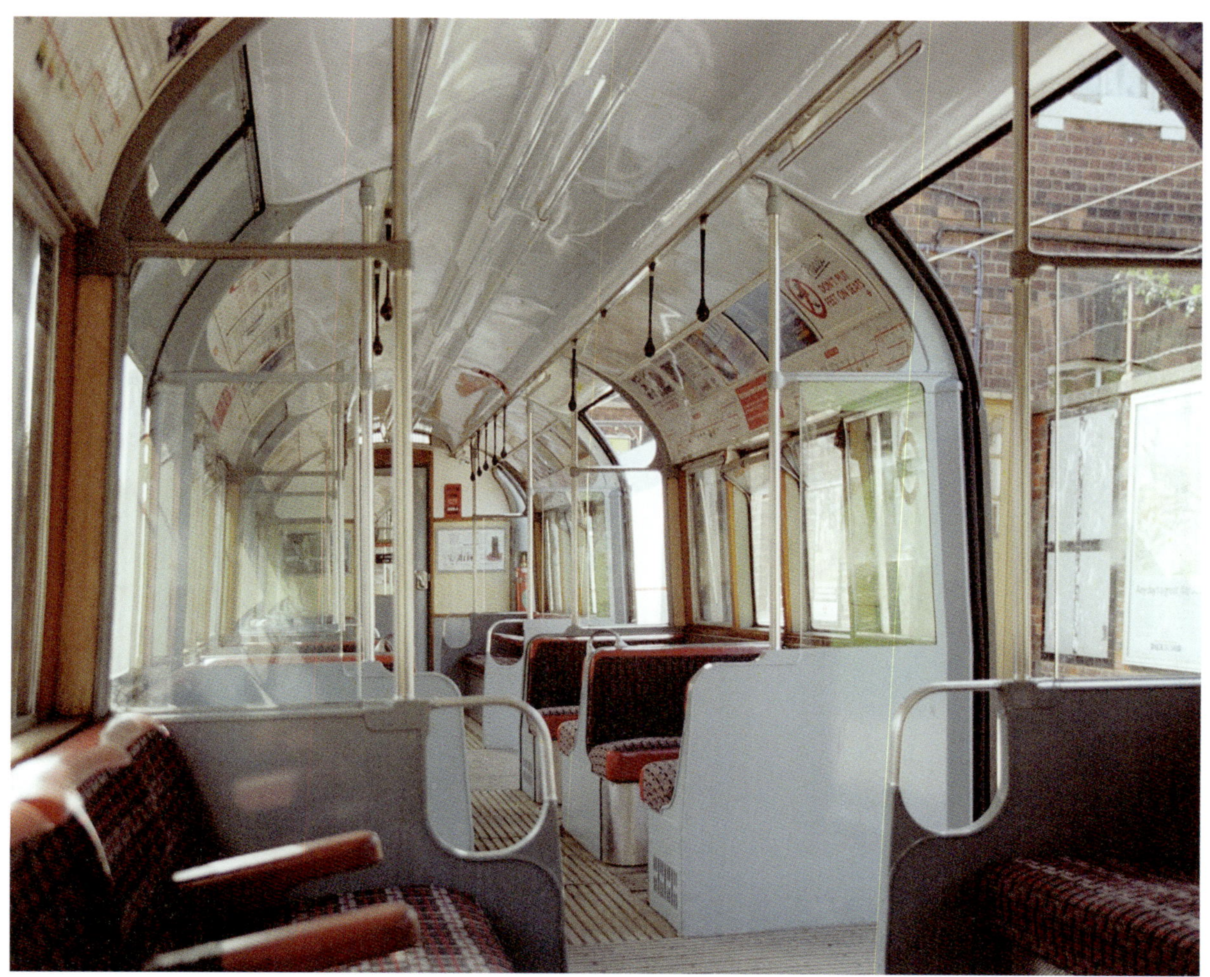

Central Line train, Epping Underground station, 1986

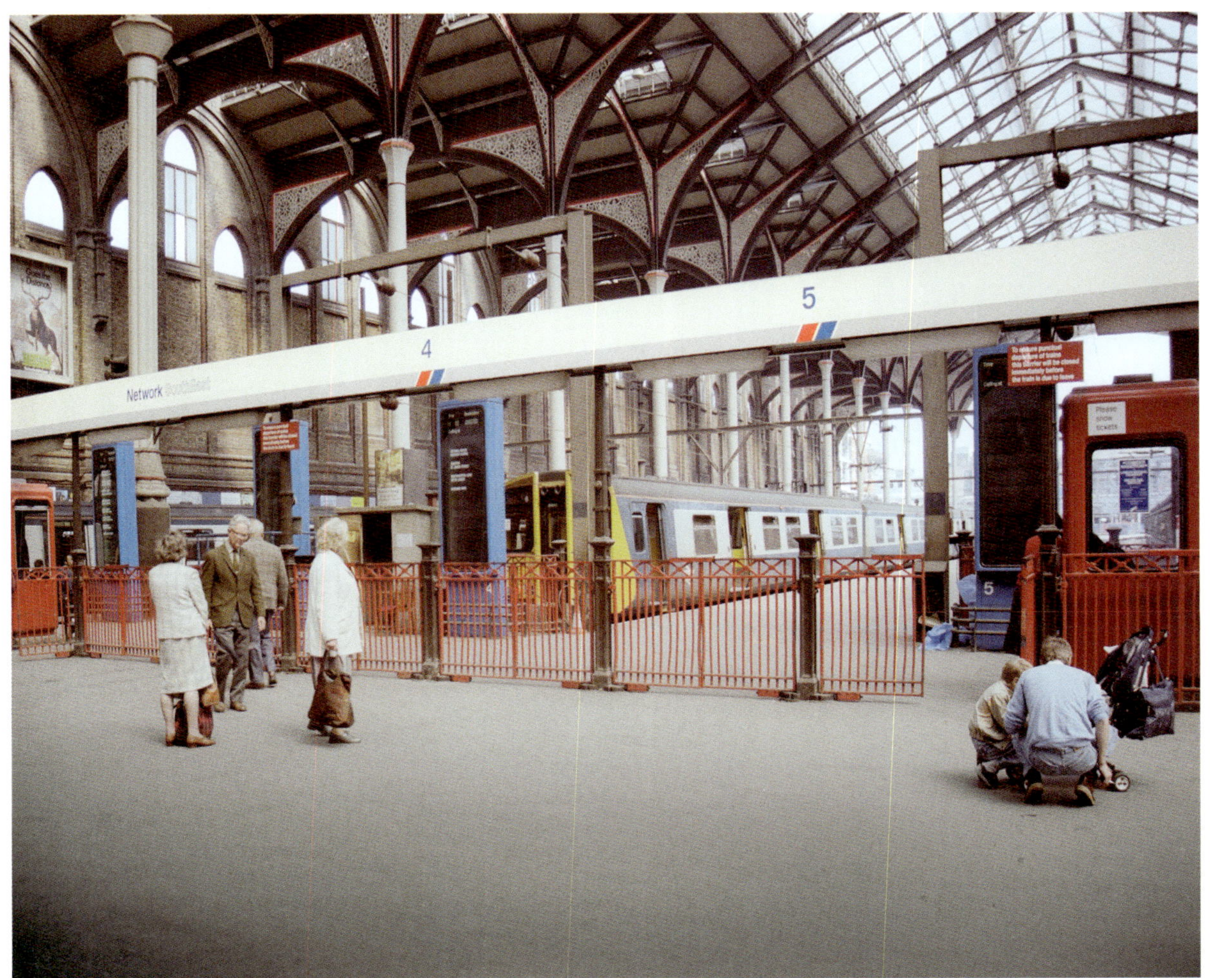

Liverpool Street station, 1987

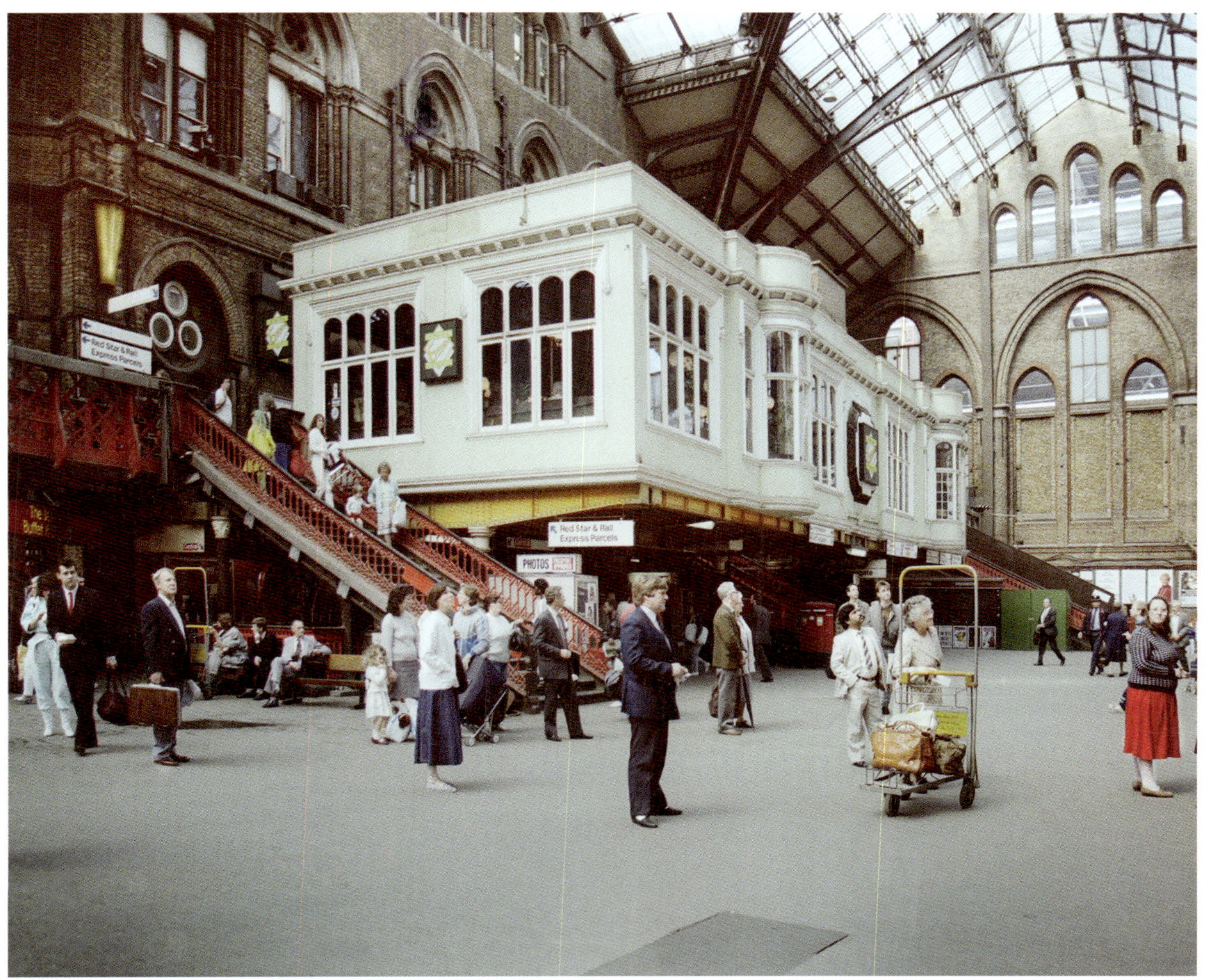

Liverpool Street station, 1987

Aldgate Underground station, 1988

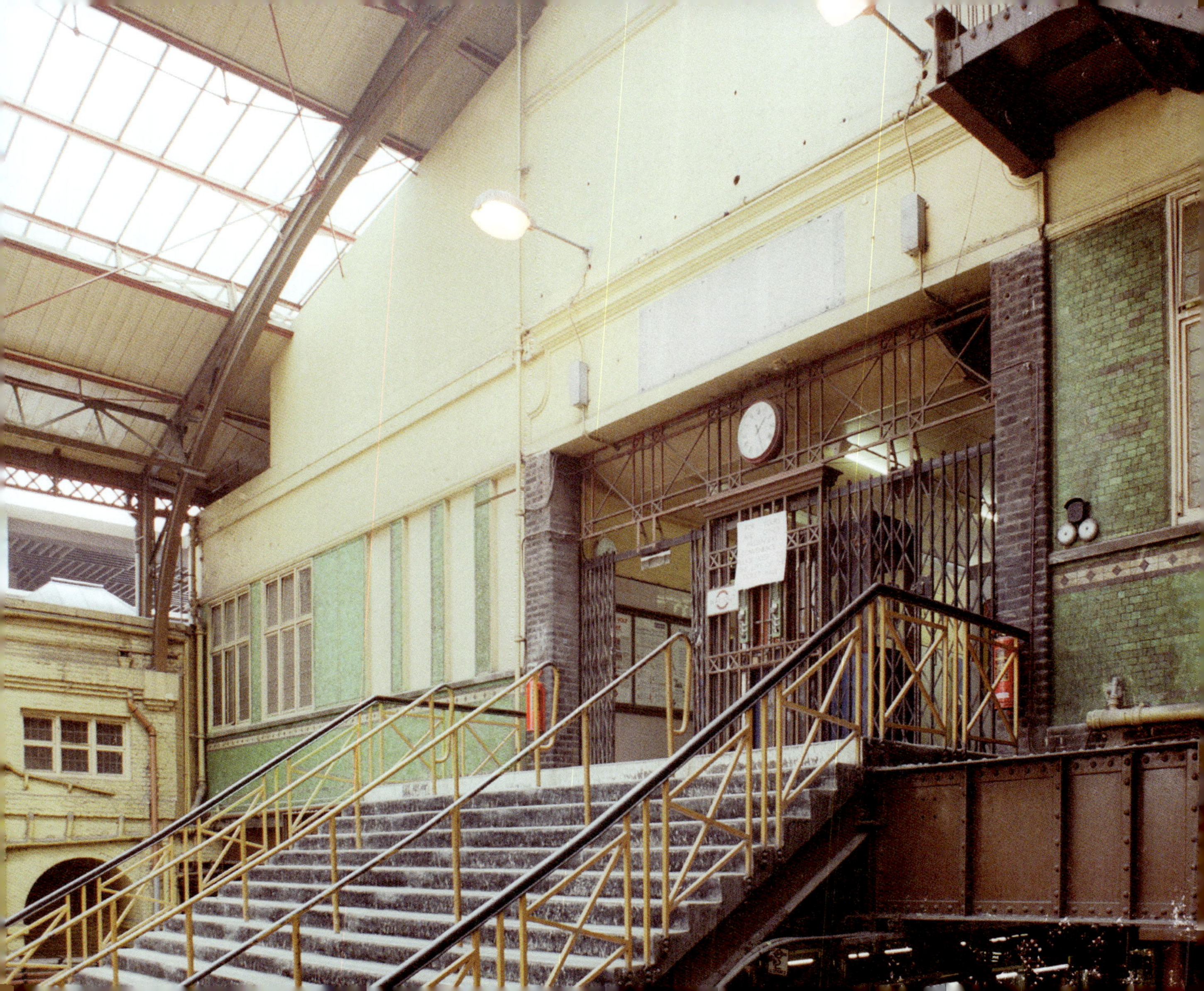

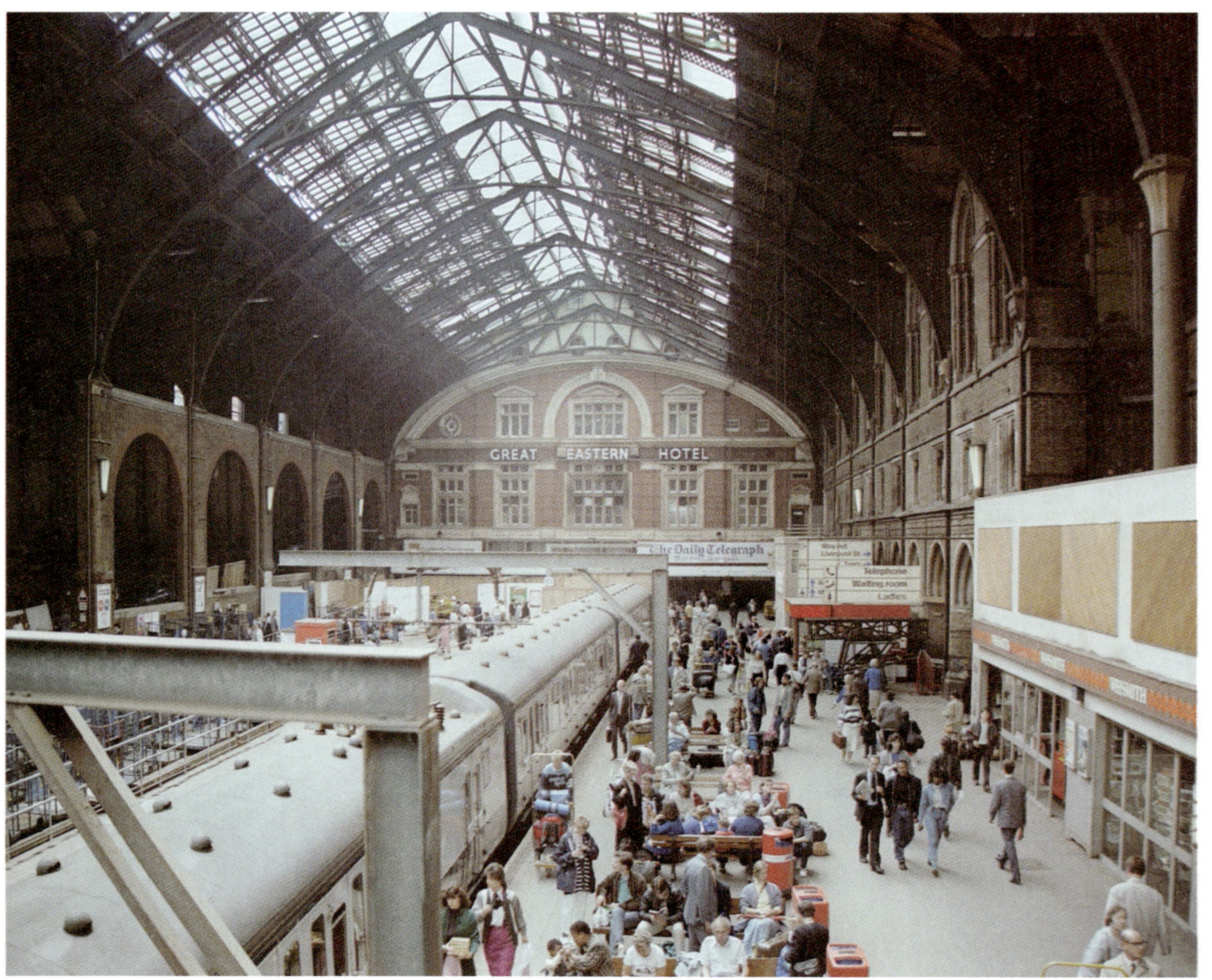

Liverpool Street station, 1987

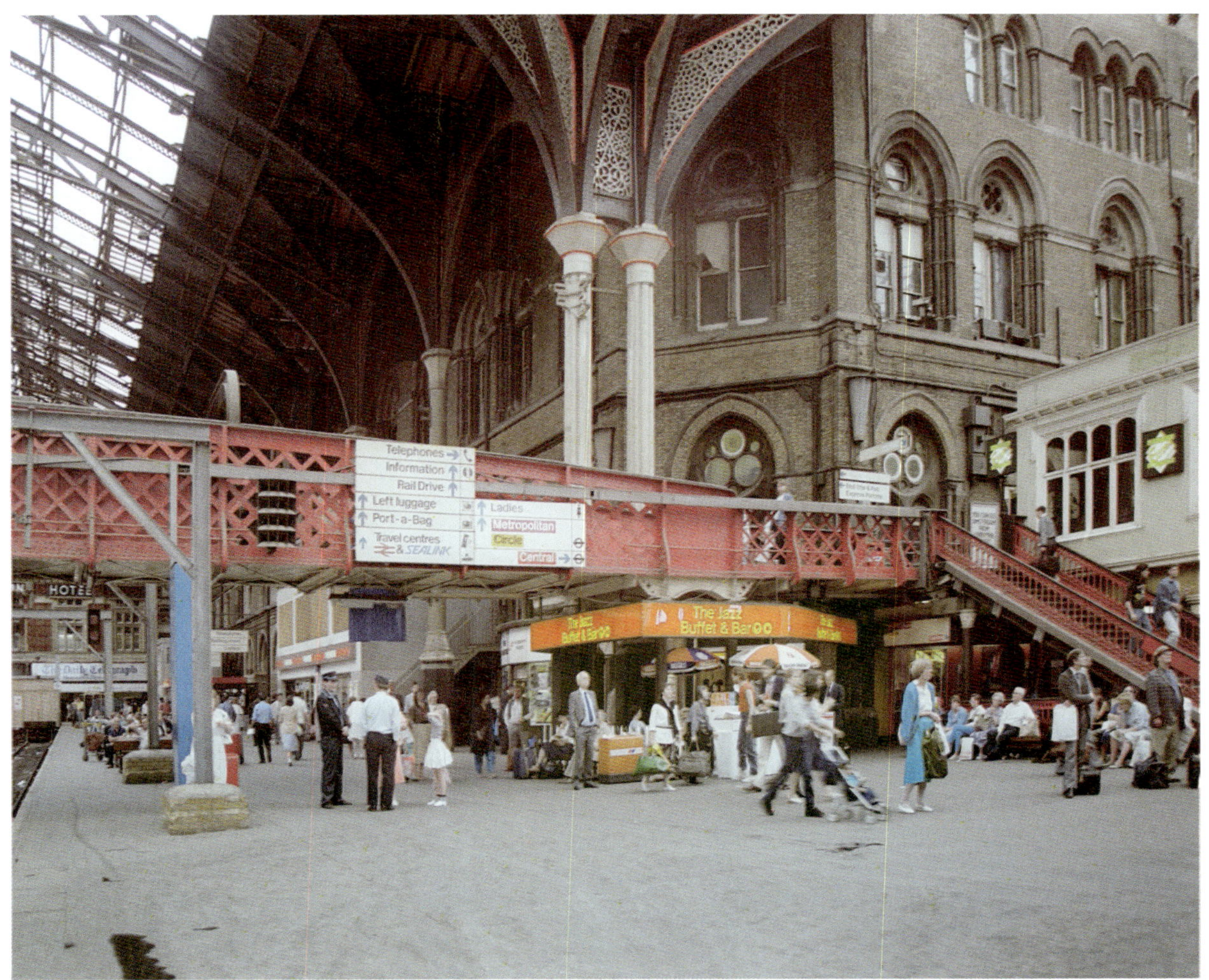

Liverpool Street station, 1987

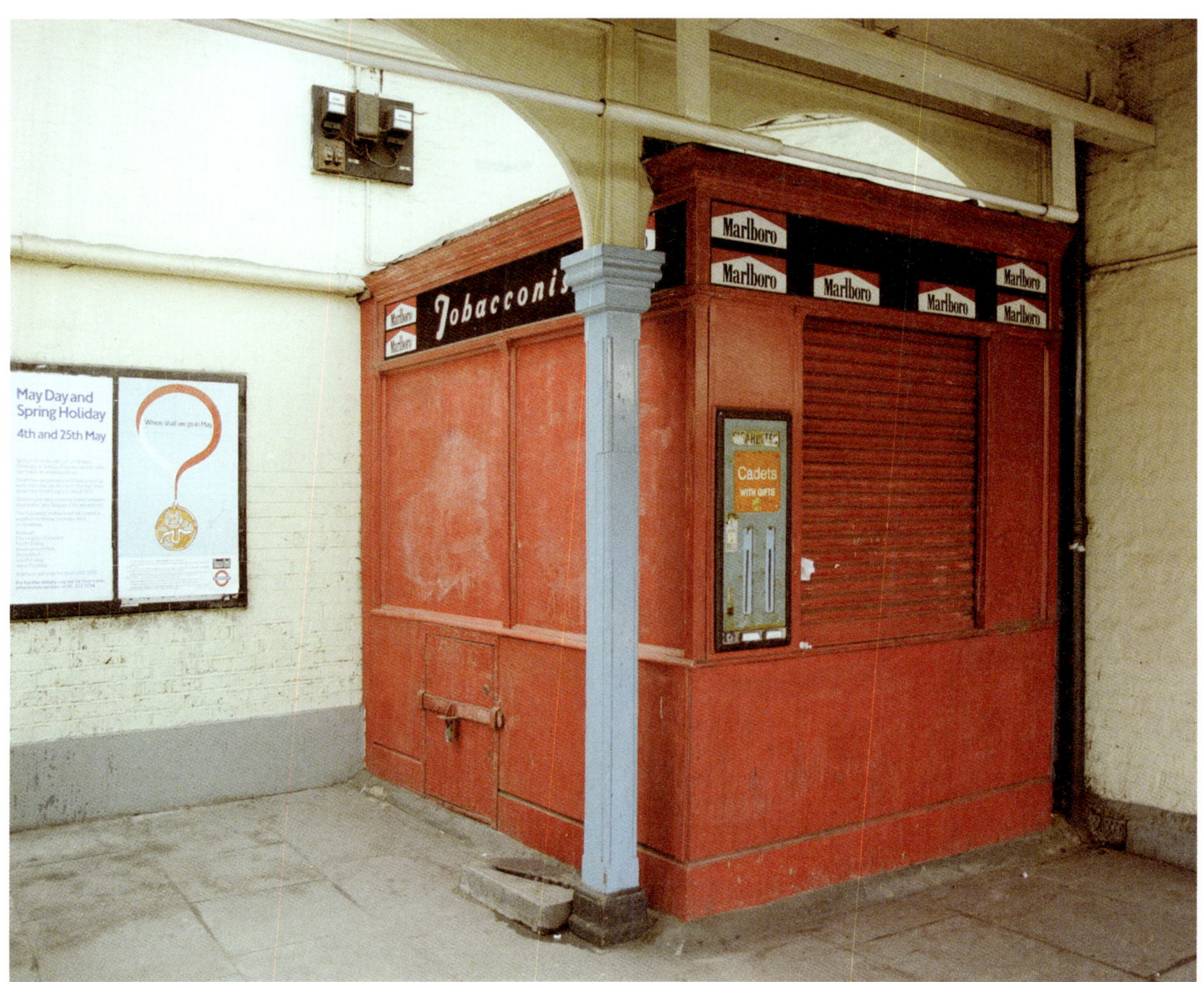

Leyton Underground station, 1987

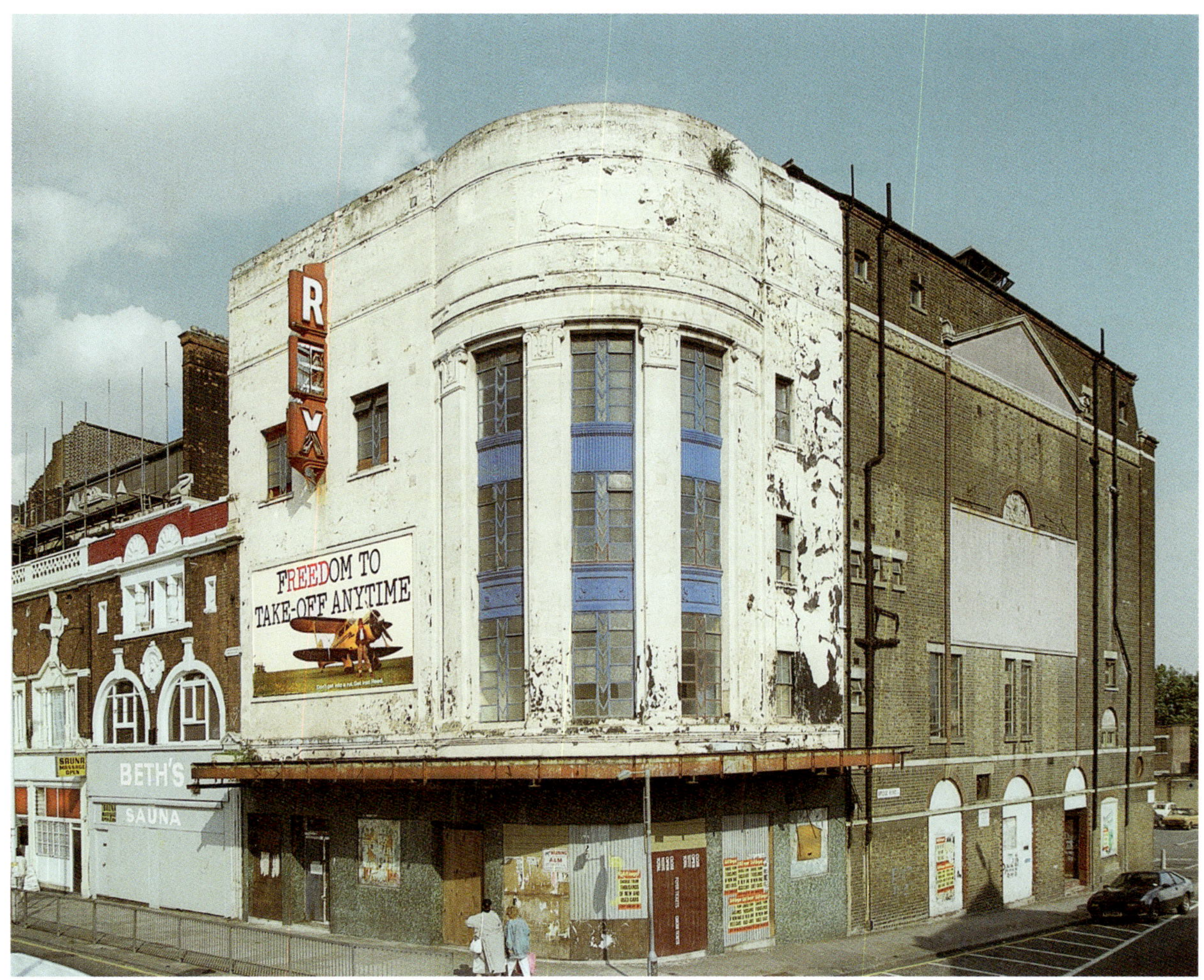

Rex Cinema, Stratford High Street, 1987

Commercial Road, 1987

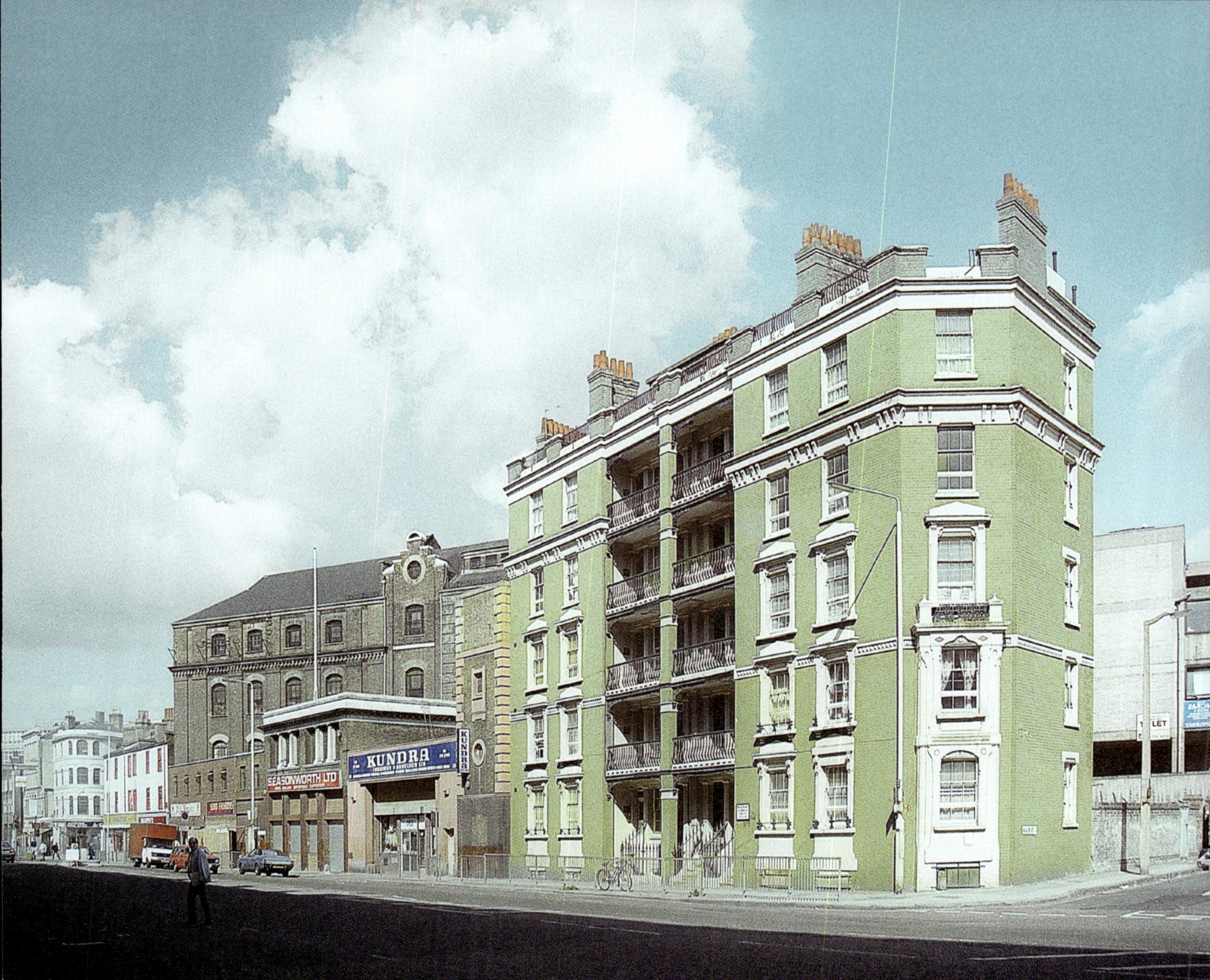
KUNDRA
SEASONWORTH LTD
TO LET

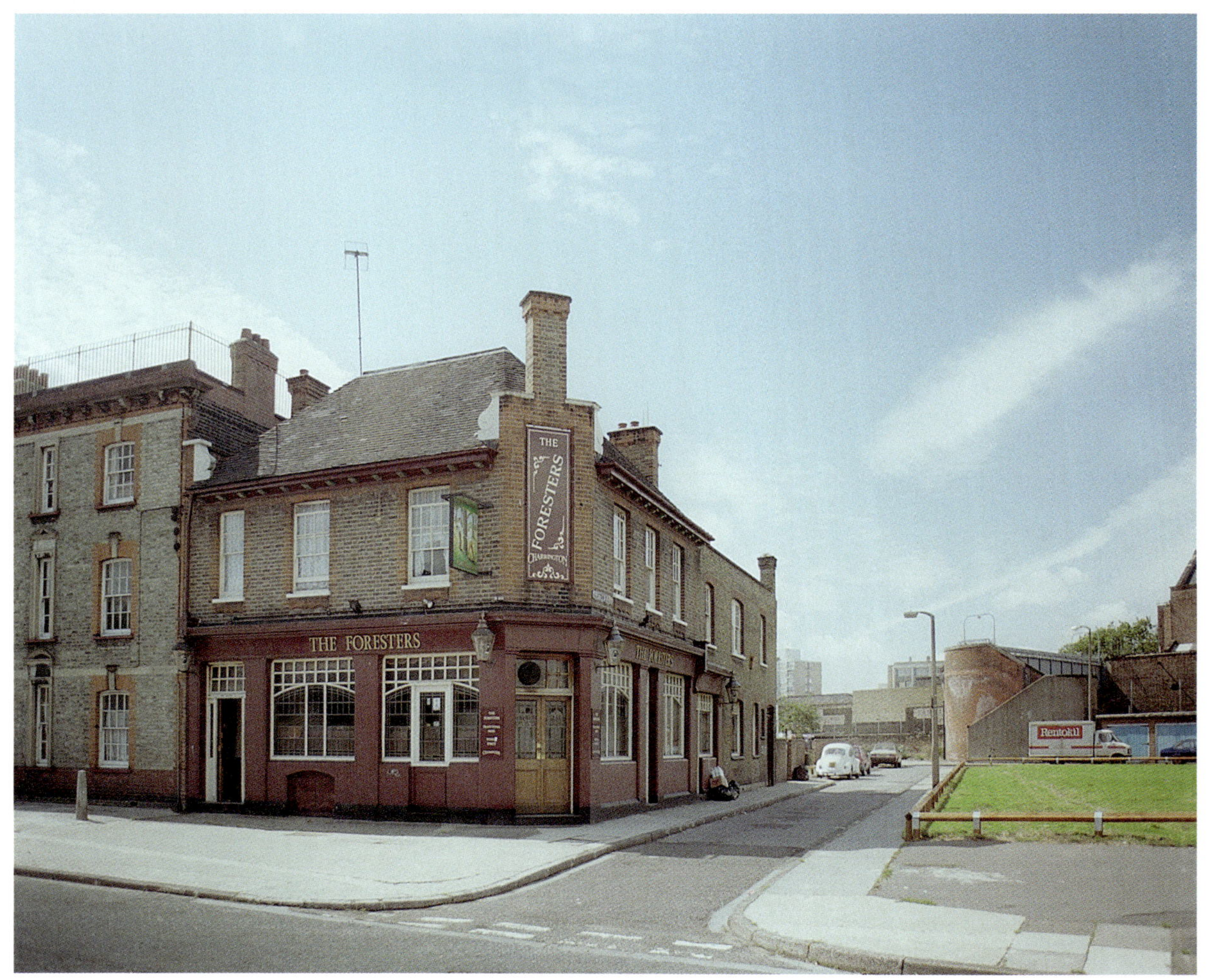

The Foresters, Clutton Street, 1989

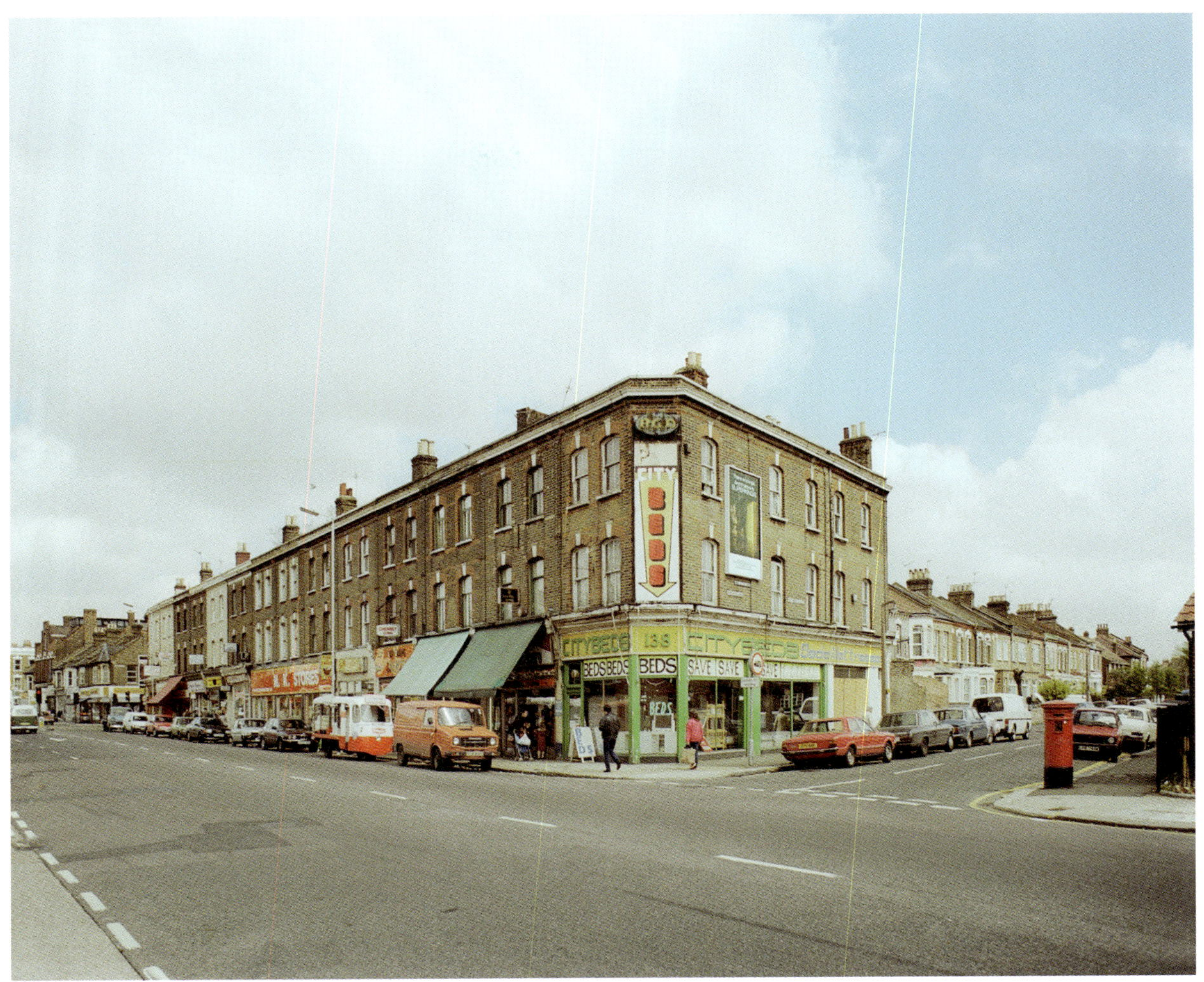

High Road Leytonstone, 1988

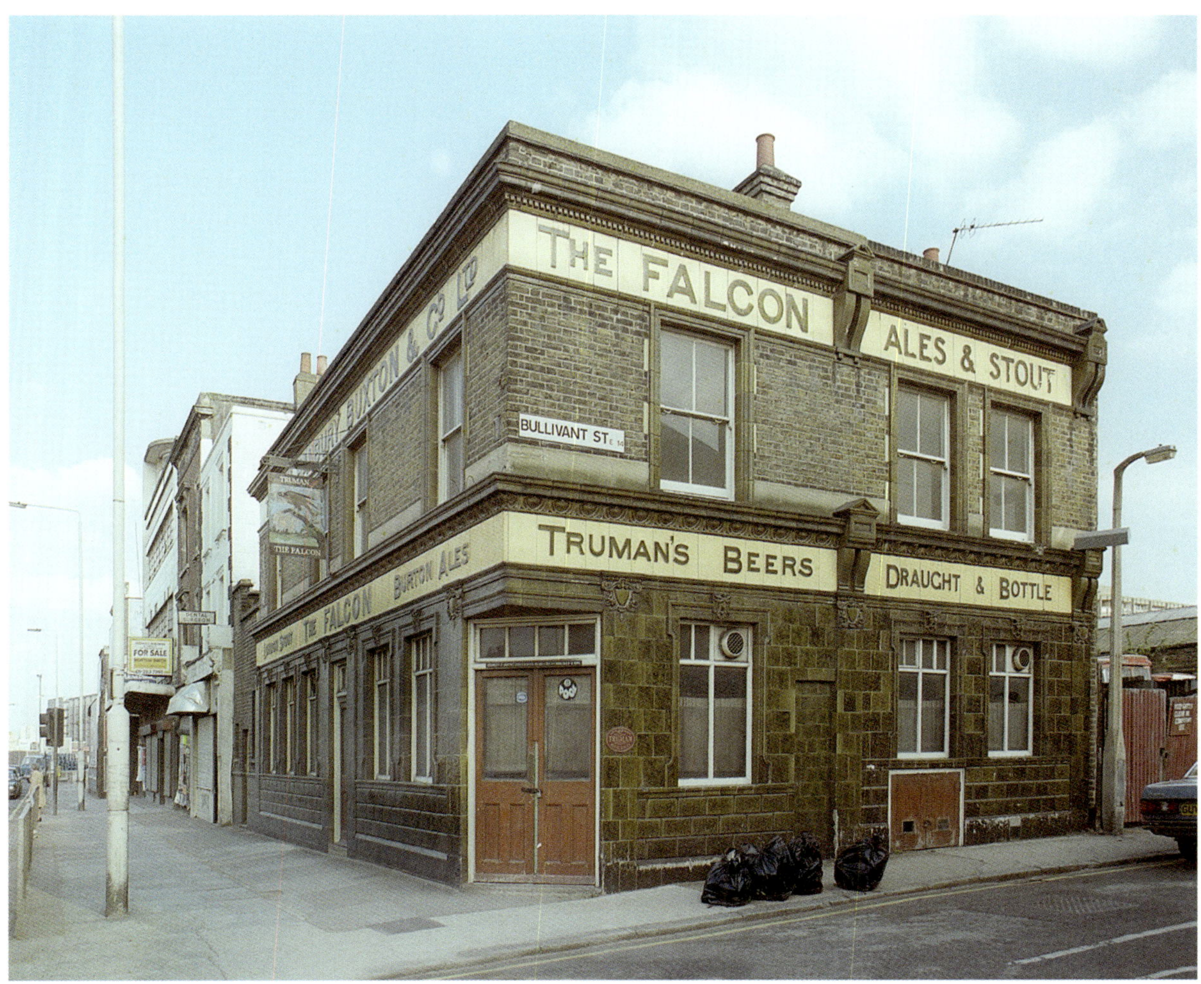

The Falcon, Bullivant Street, 1988

Potters Fields, 1987

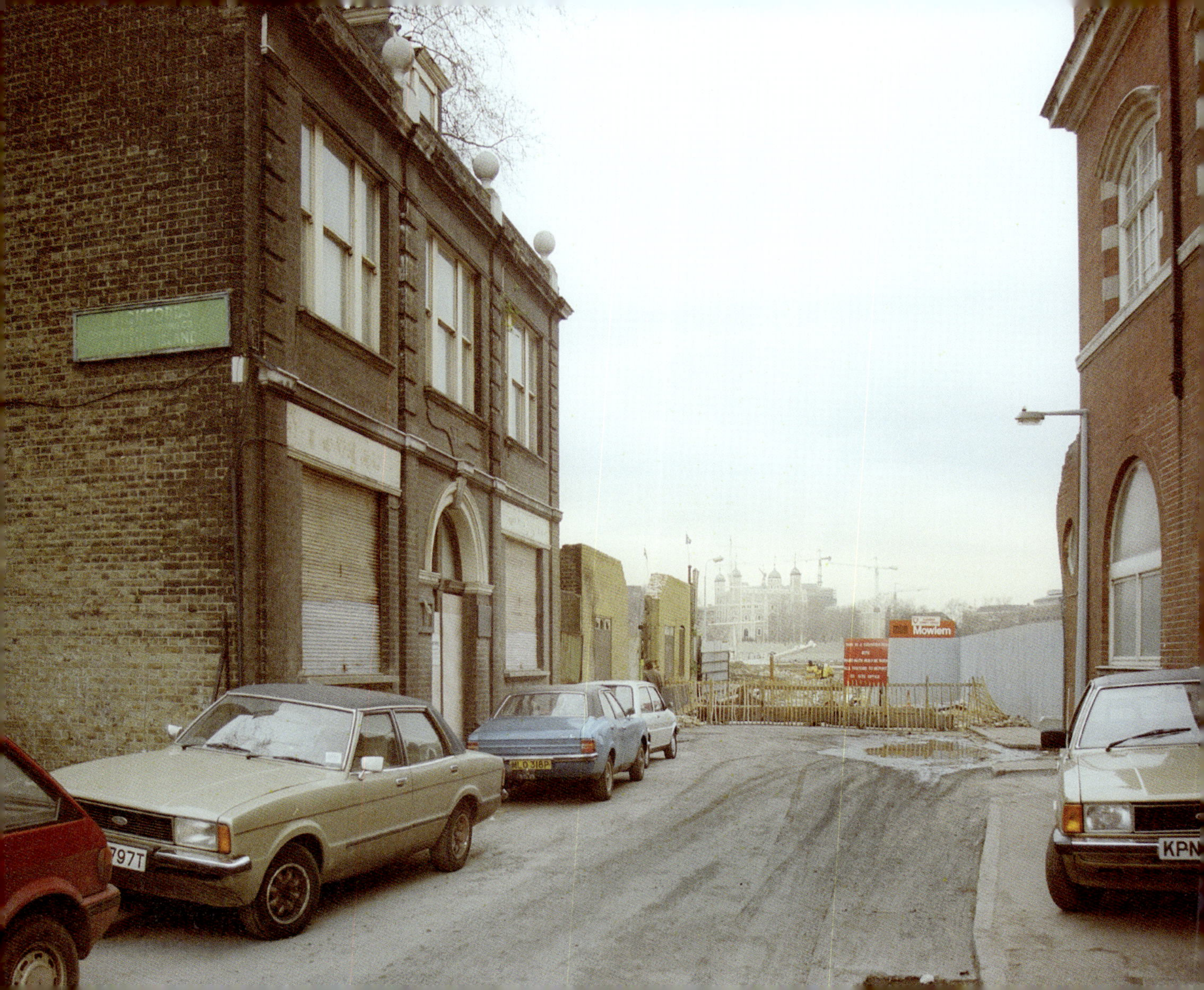

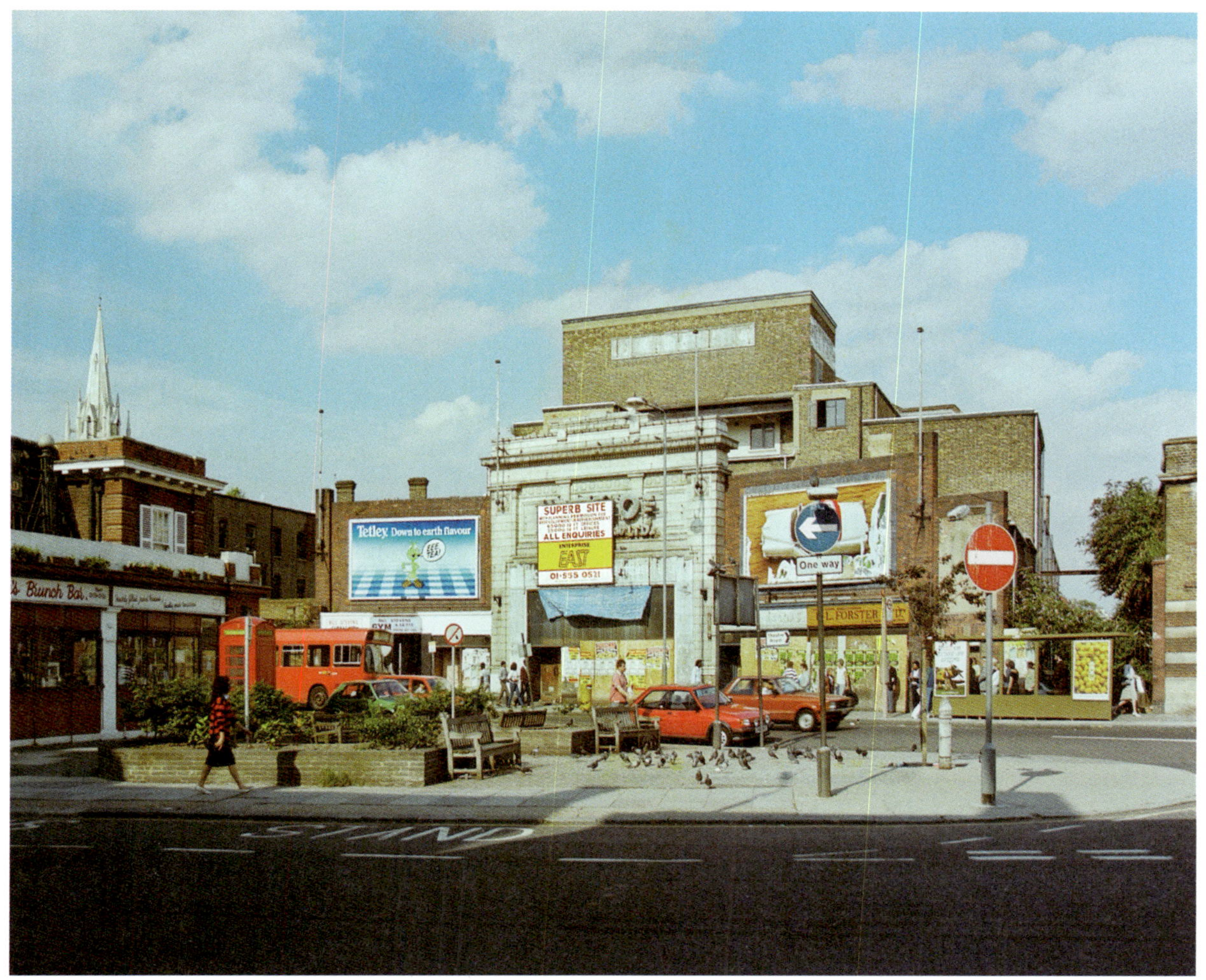

Tramway Avenue, 1987

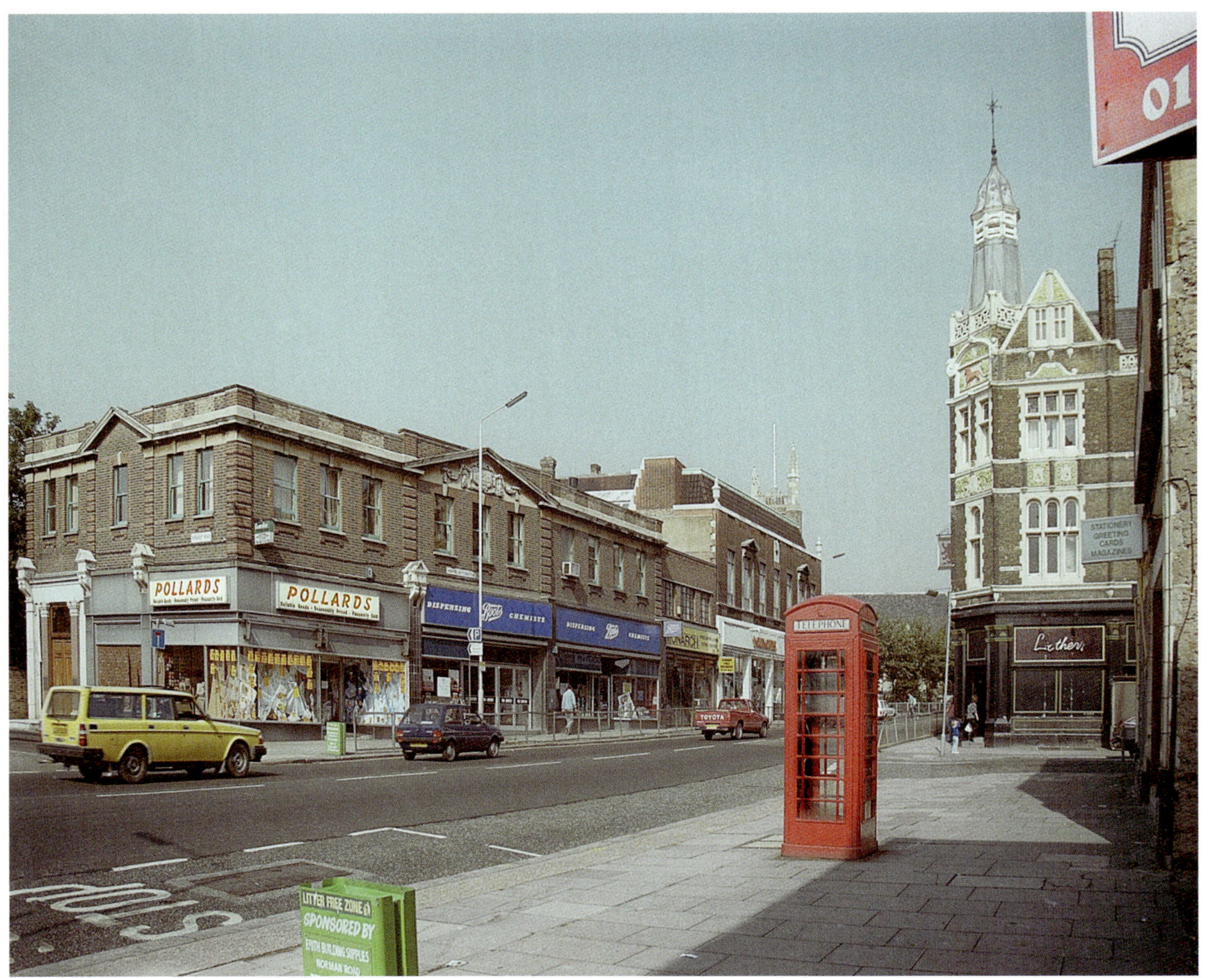

High Road Leytonstone, 1987

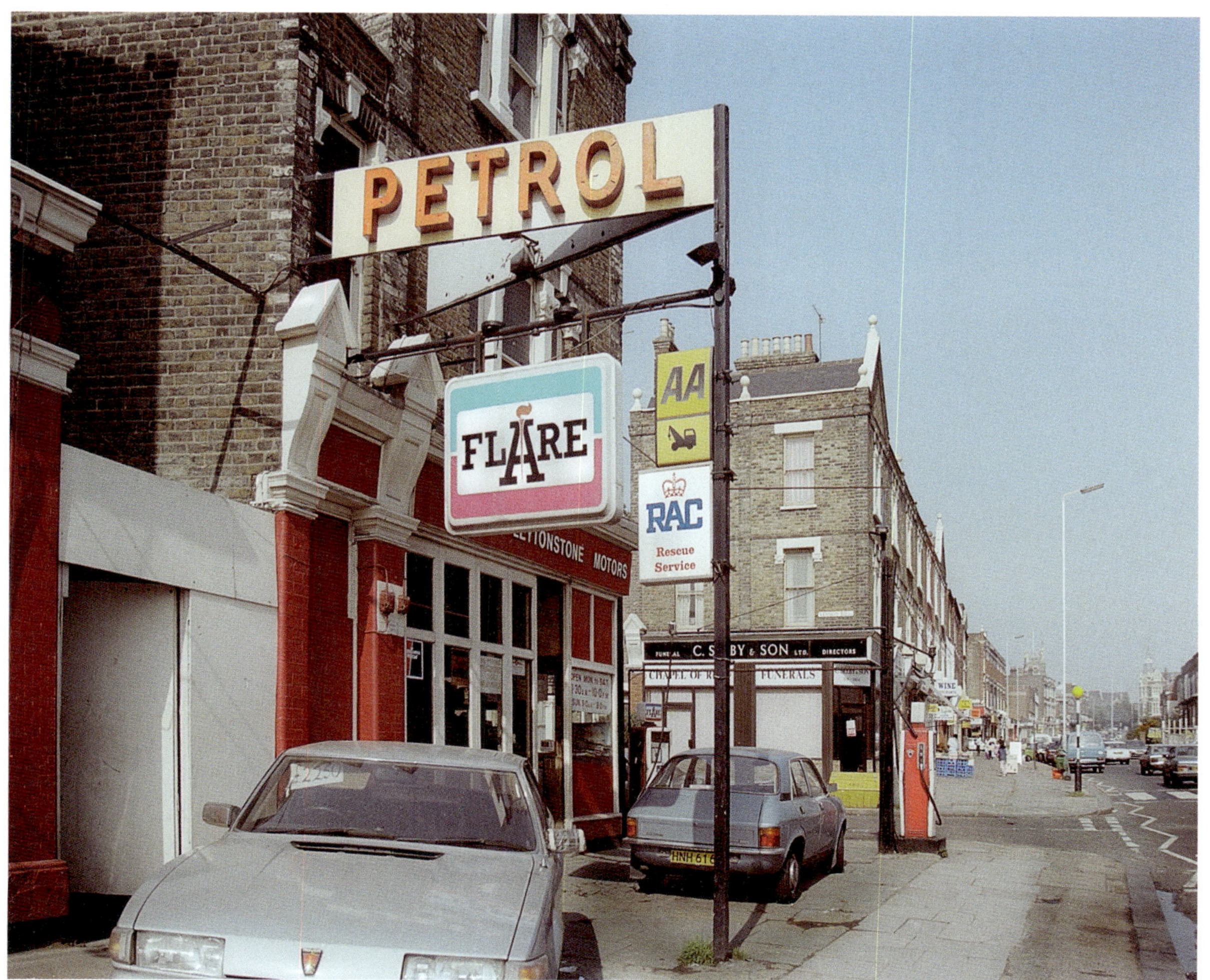

High Road Leytonstone, 1987

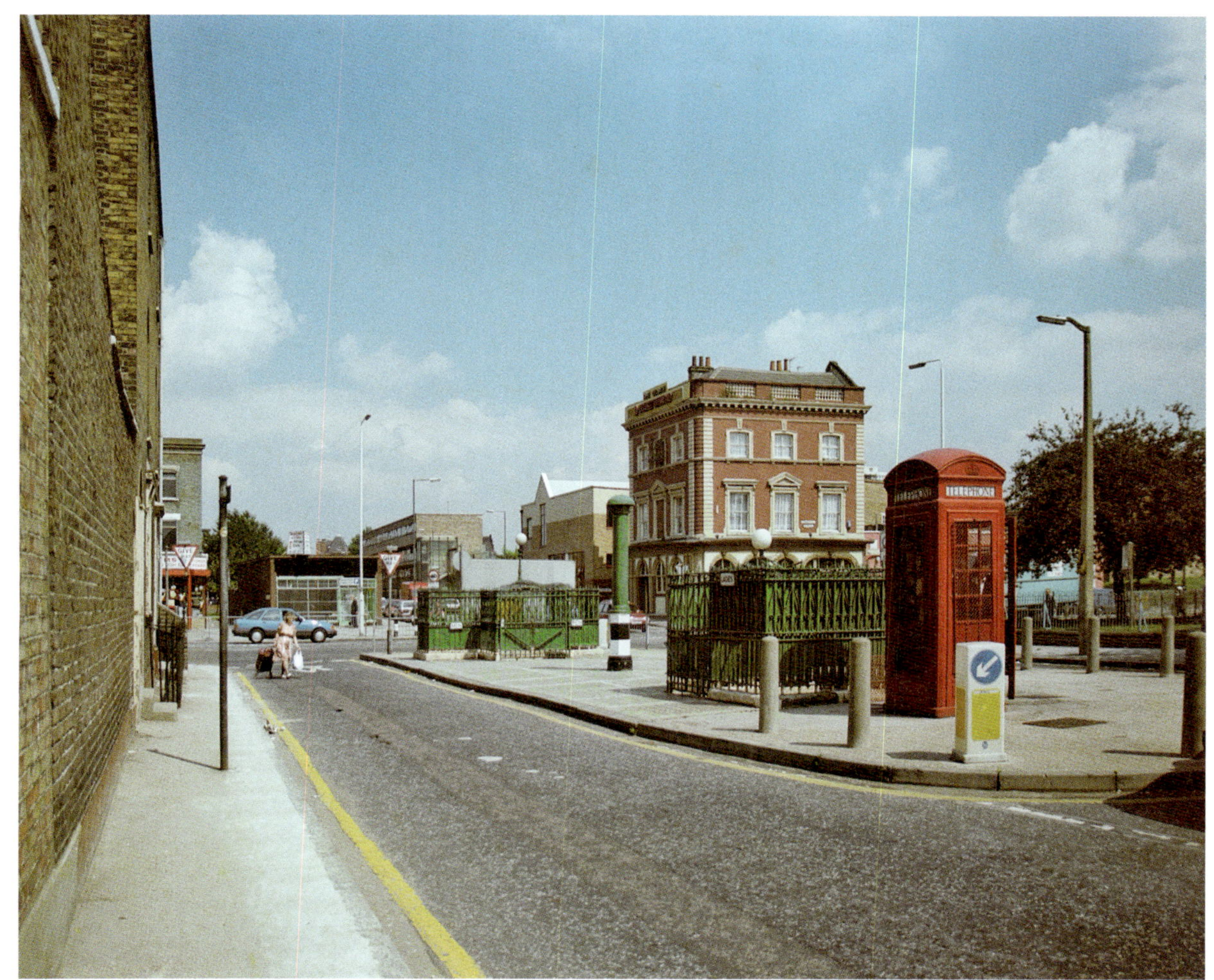

Sutton Street, 1987

The White Hart, Narrow Street, 1988

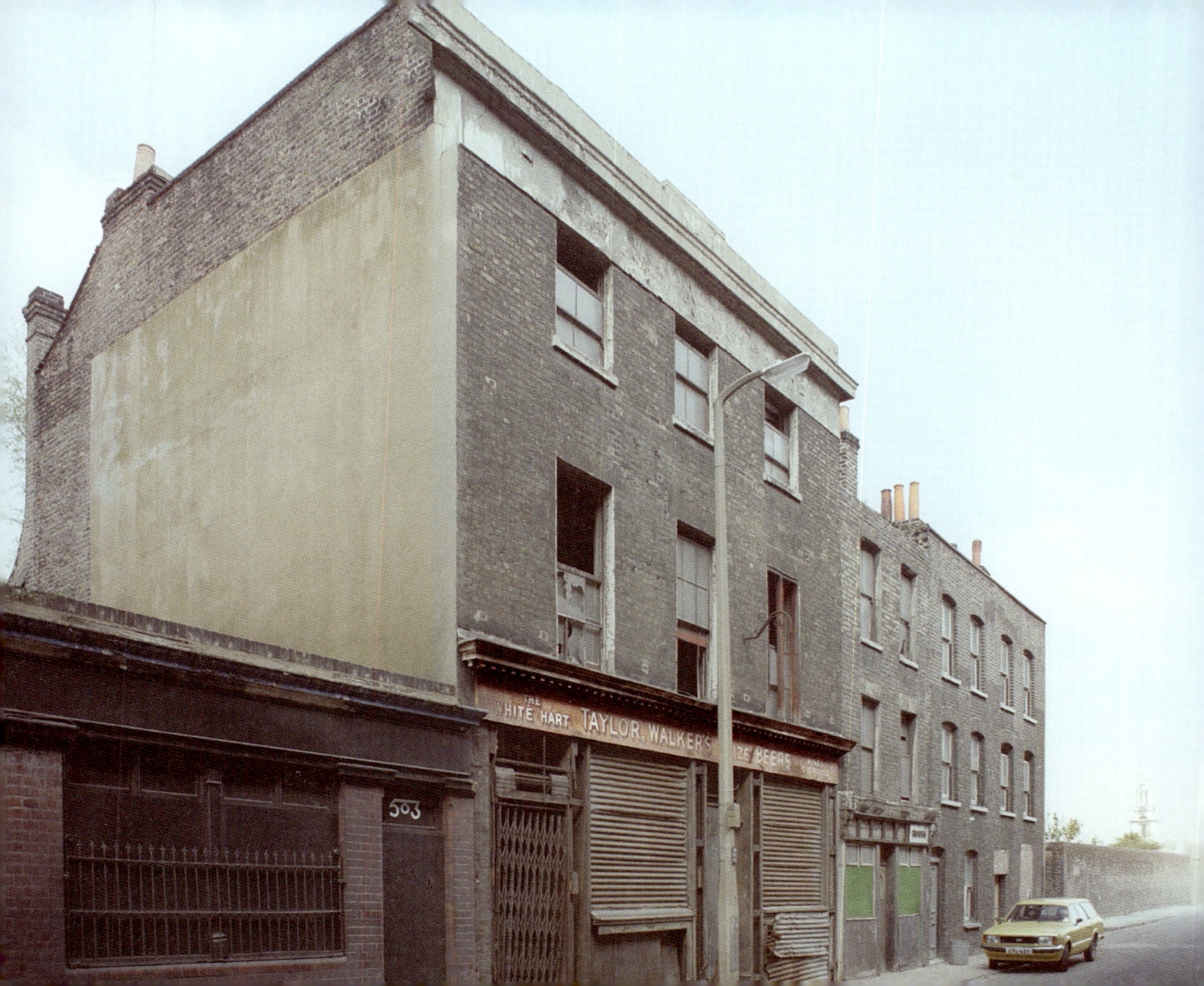
THE
WHITE HART   TAYLOR, WALKER'S   PRIZE BEERS
503

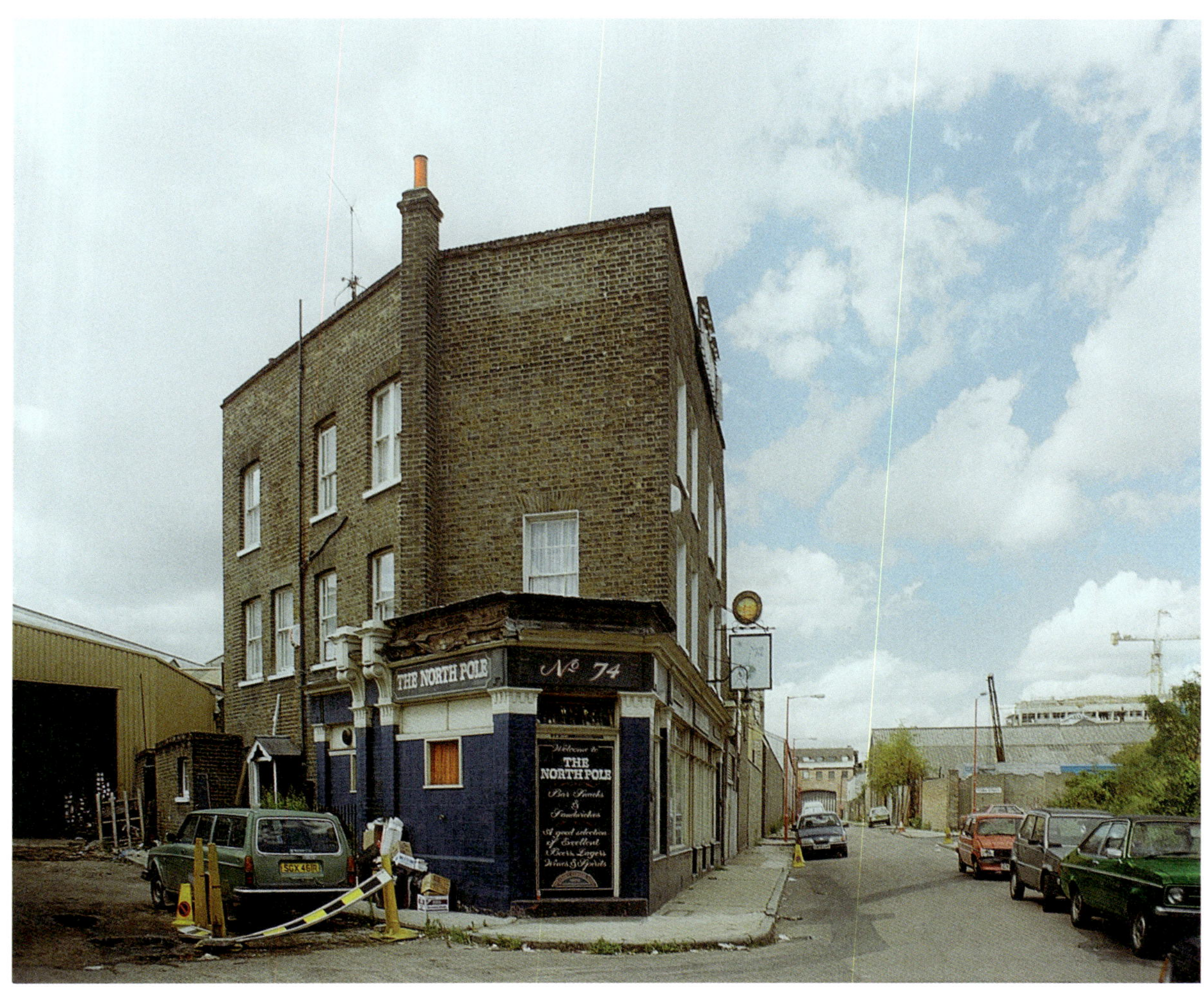

The North Pole, Manilla Street, 1989

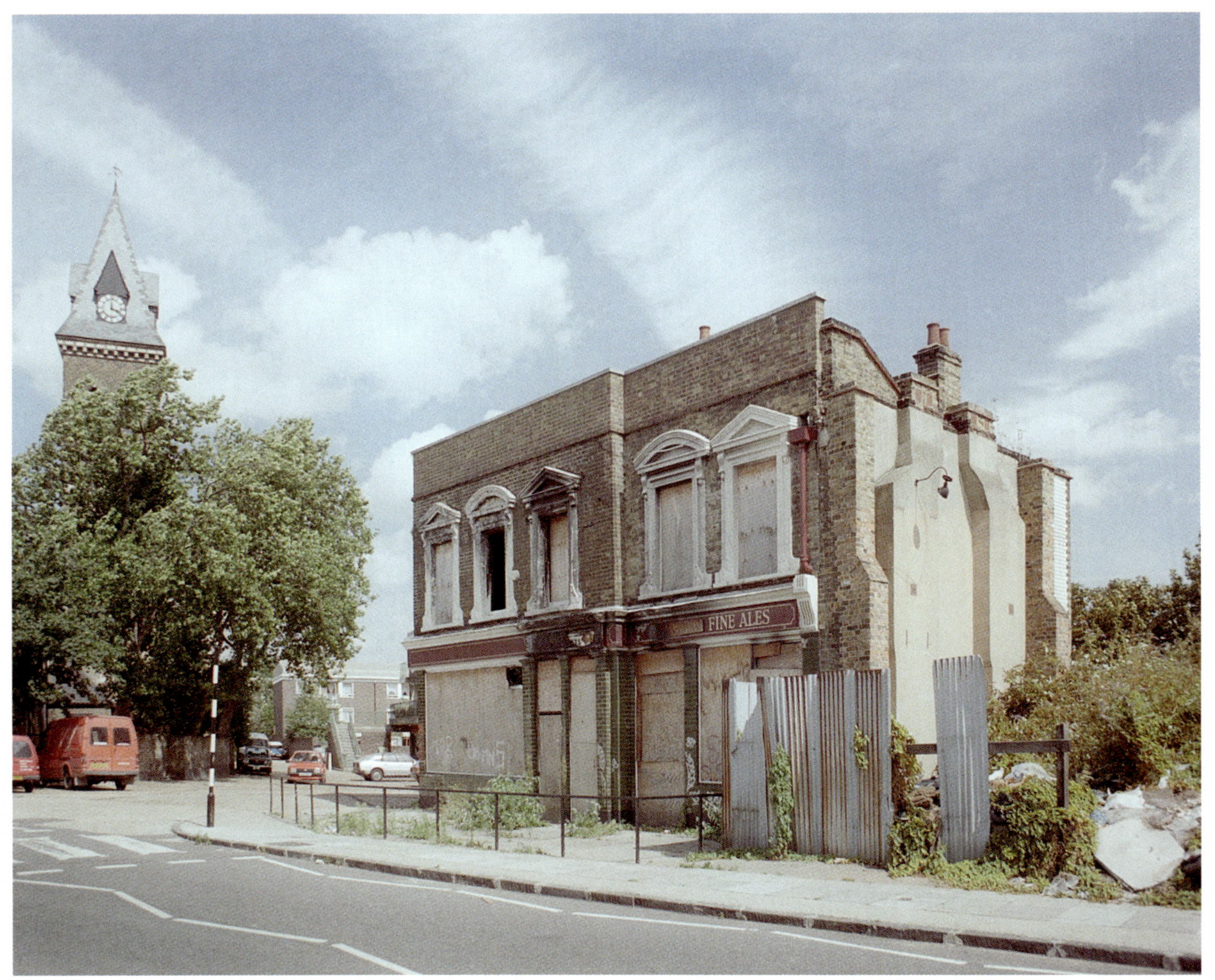

St Leonards Road, 1989

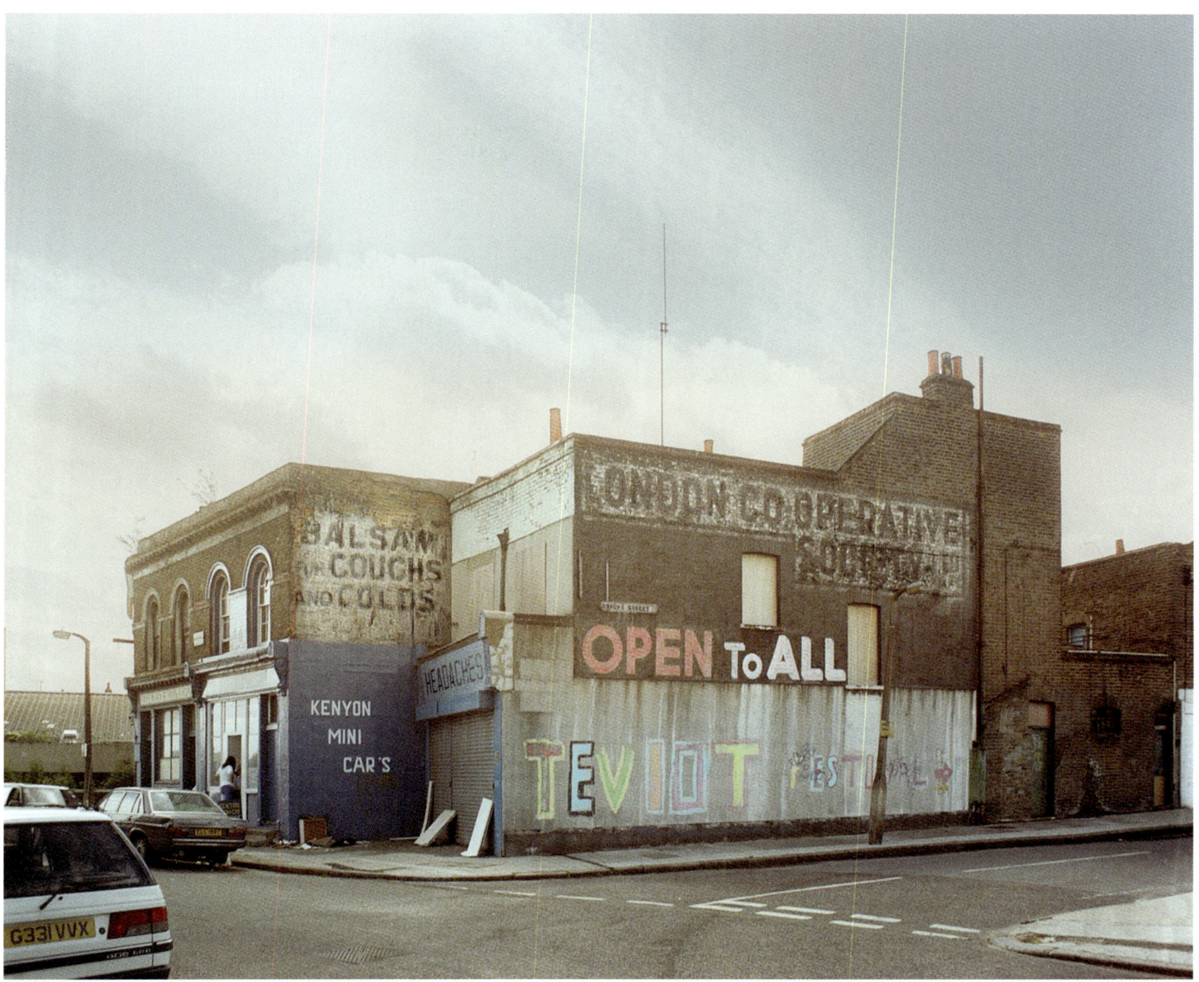

St Leonards Road, 1989

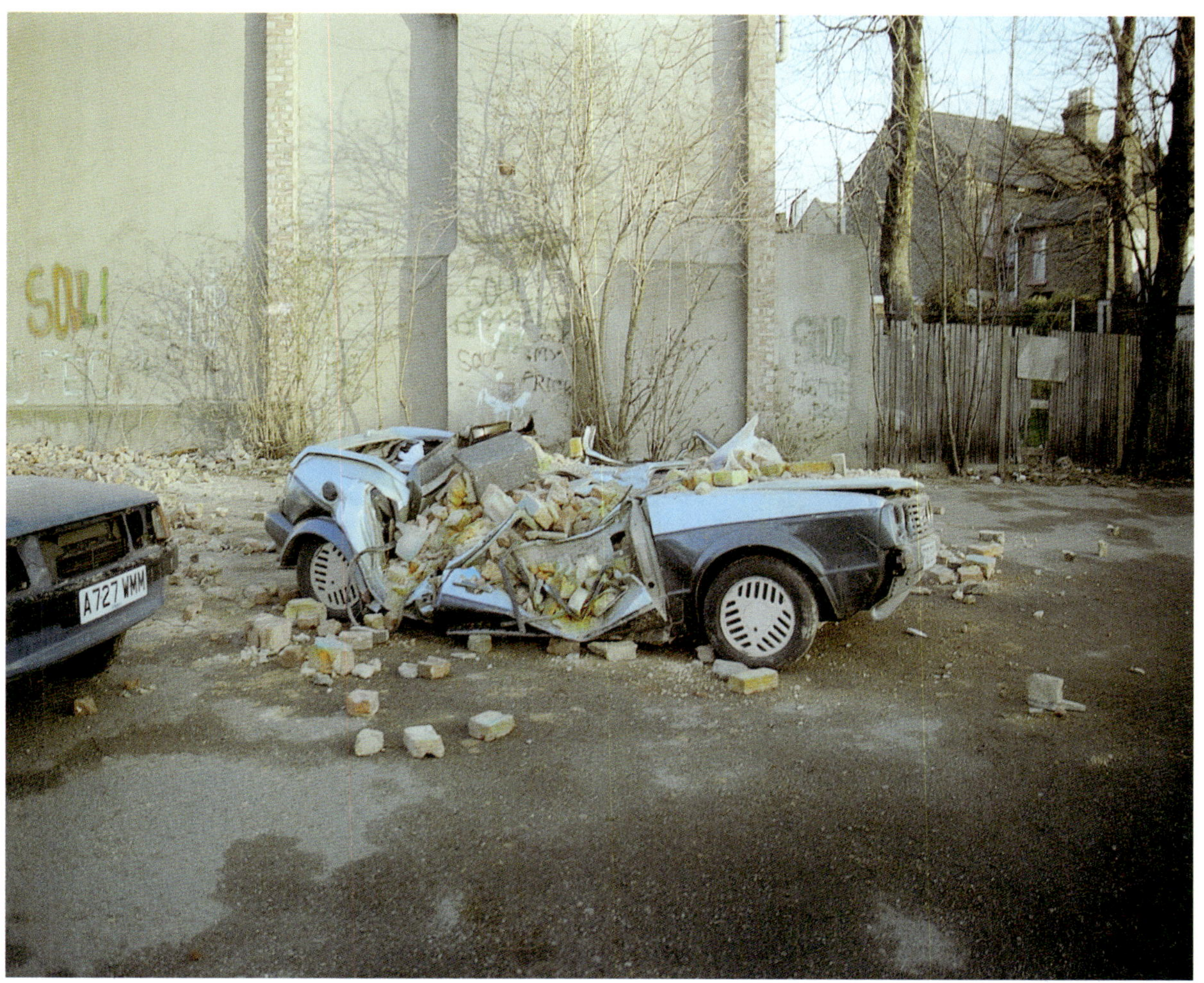

Station Road, Leyton, 1987

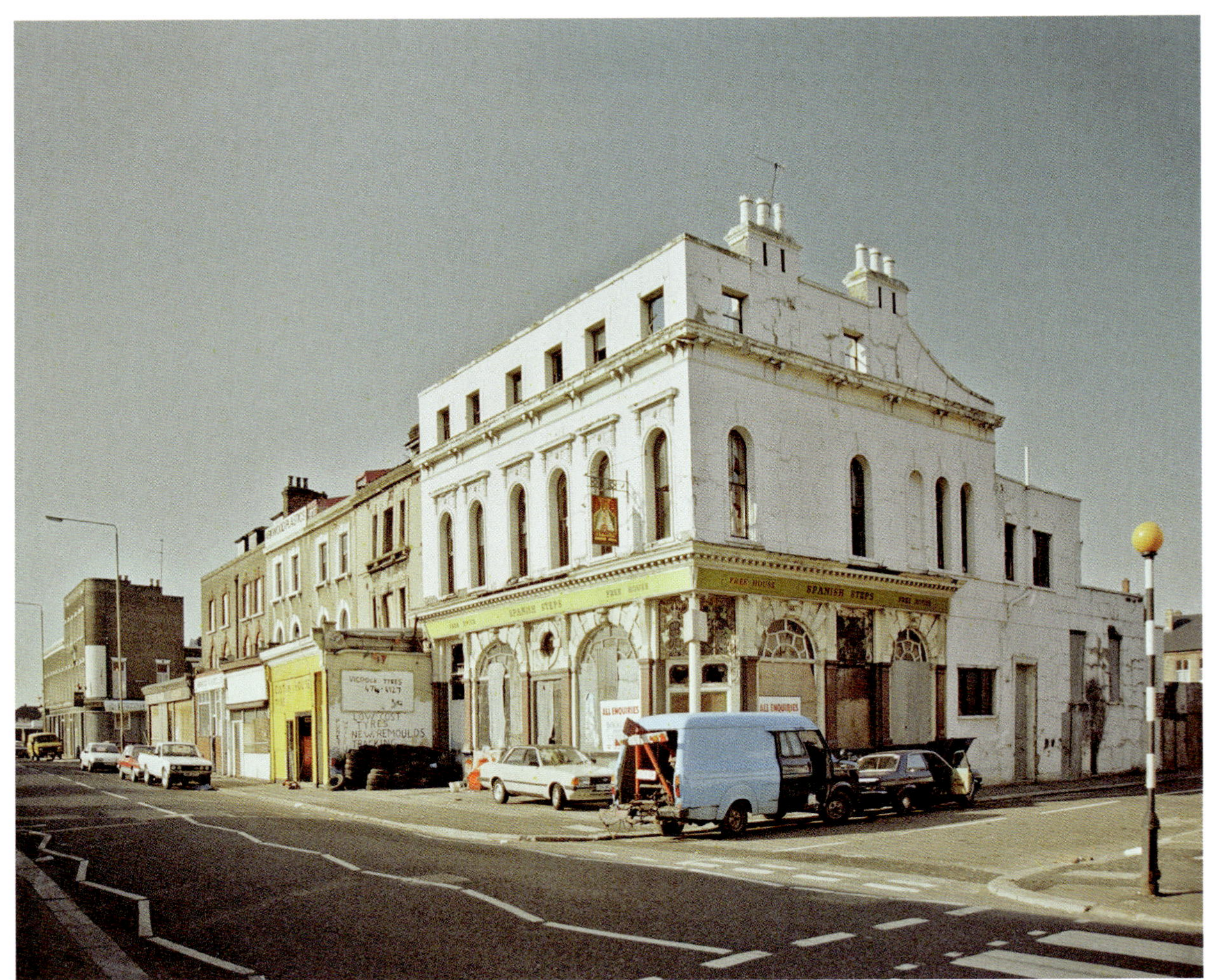

Spanish Steps, Victoria Dock Road, 1986

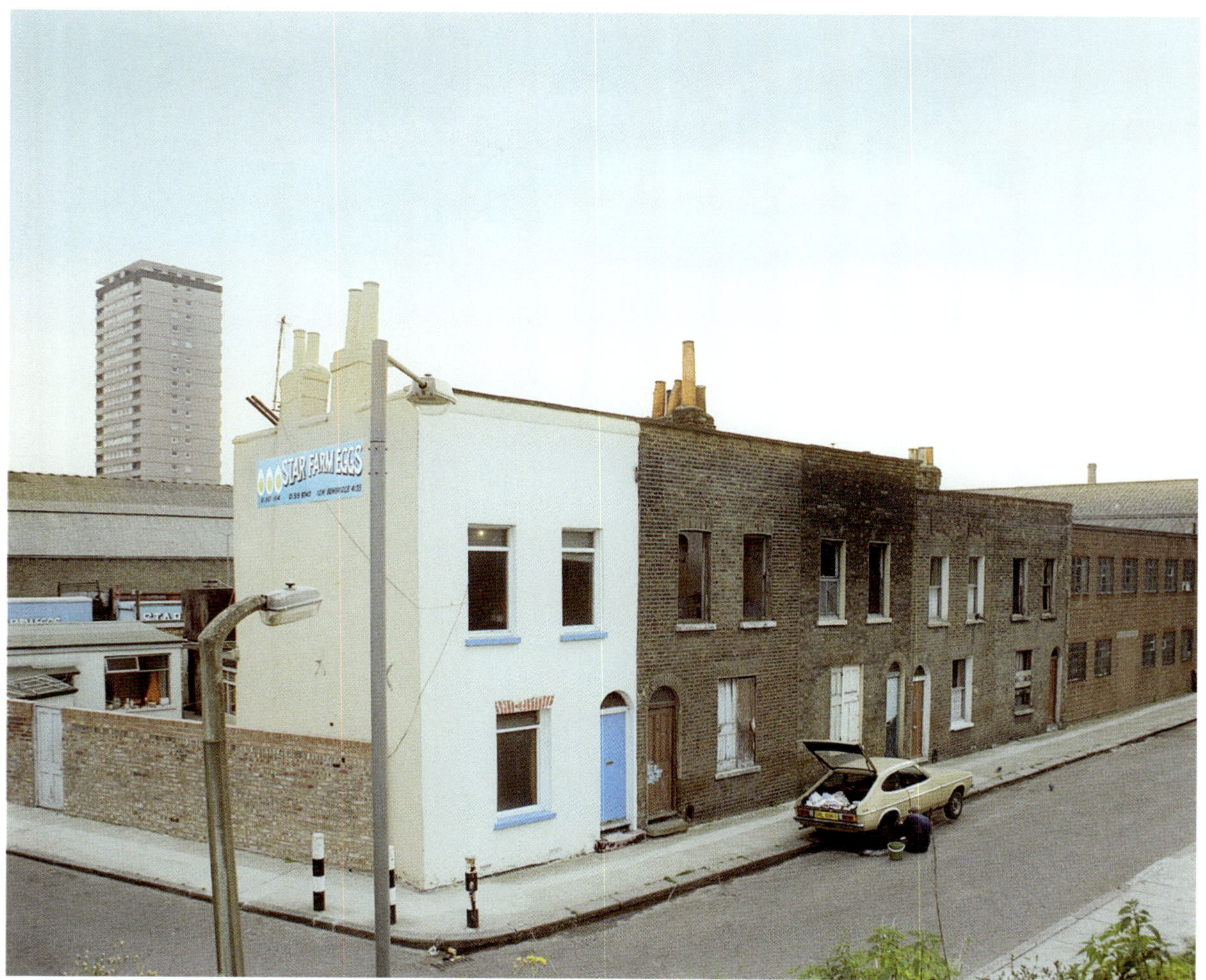

Cuba Street, 1988

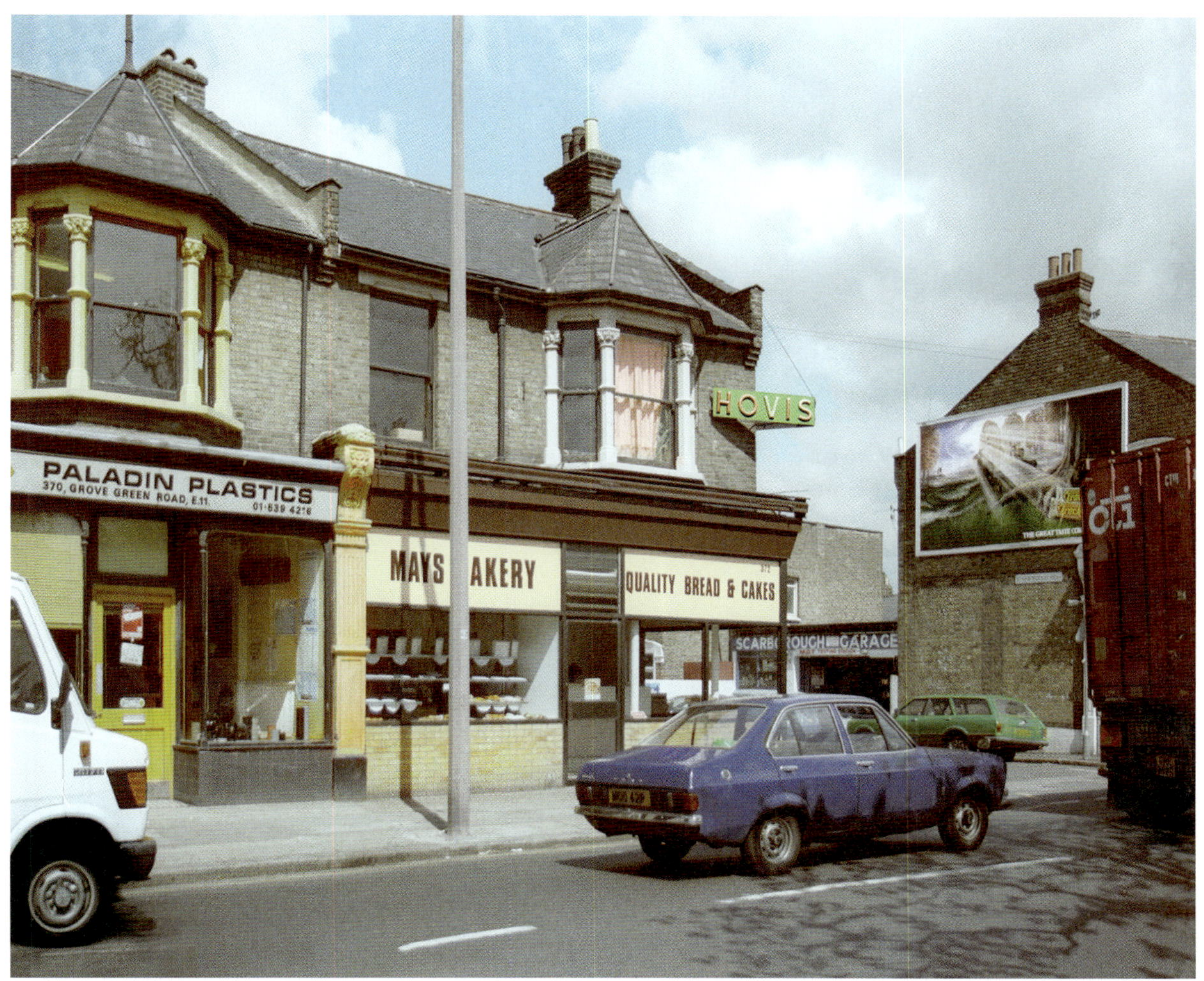

May's Bakery, Grove Green Road, 1987

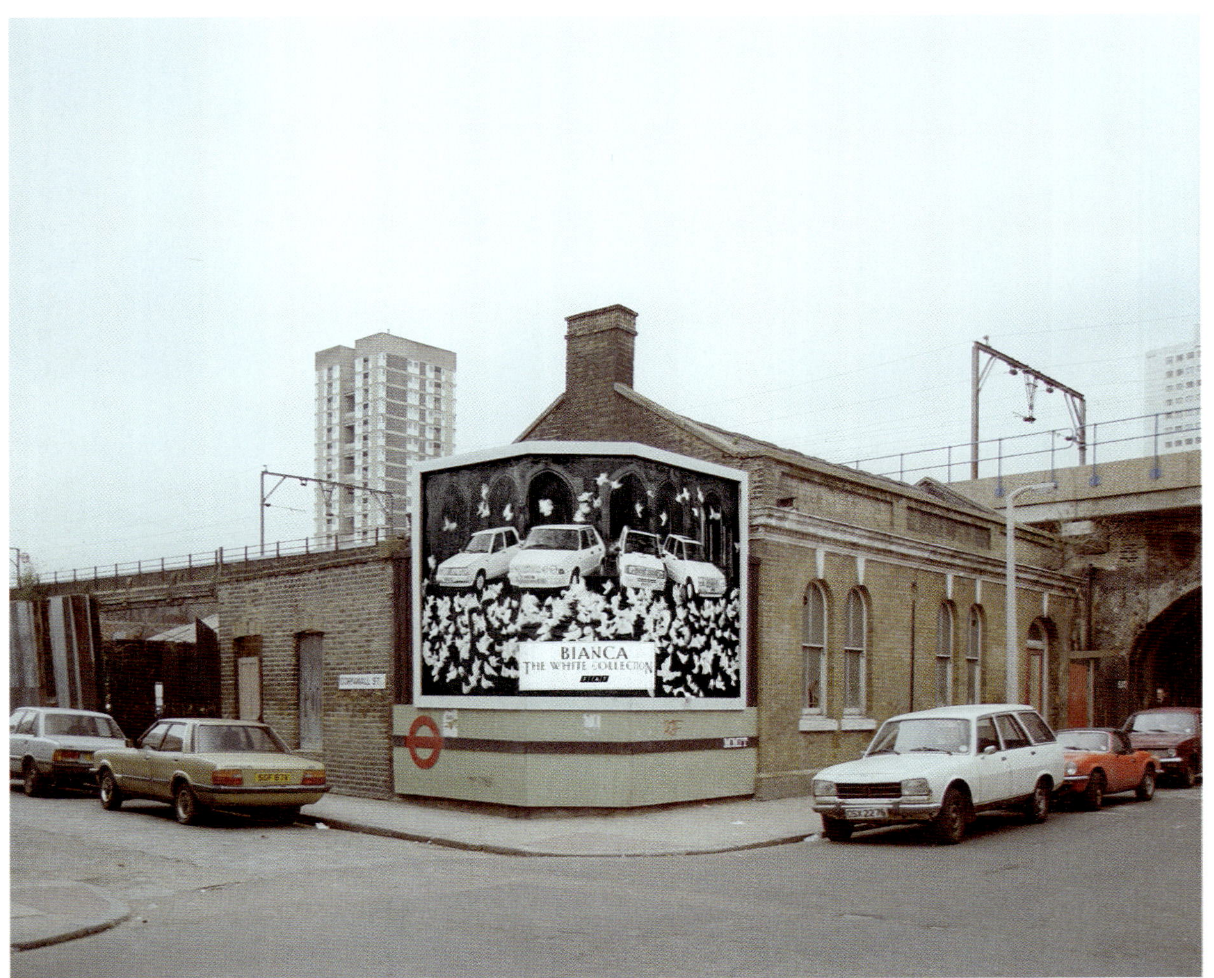

Shadwell station, Cornwall Street, 1987

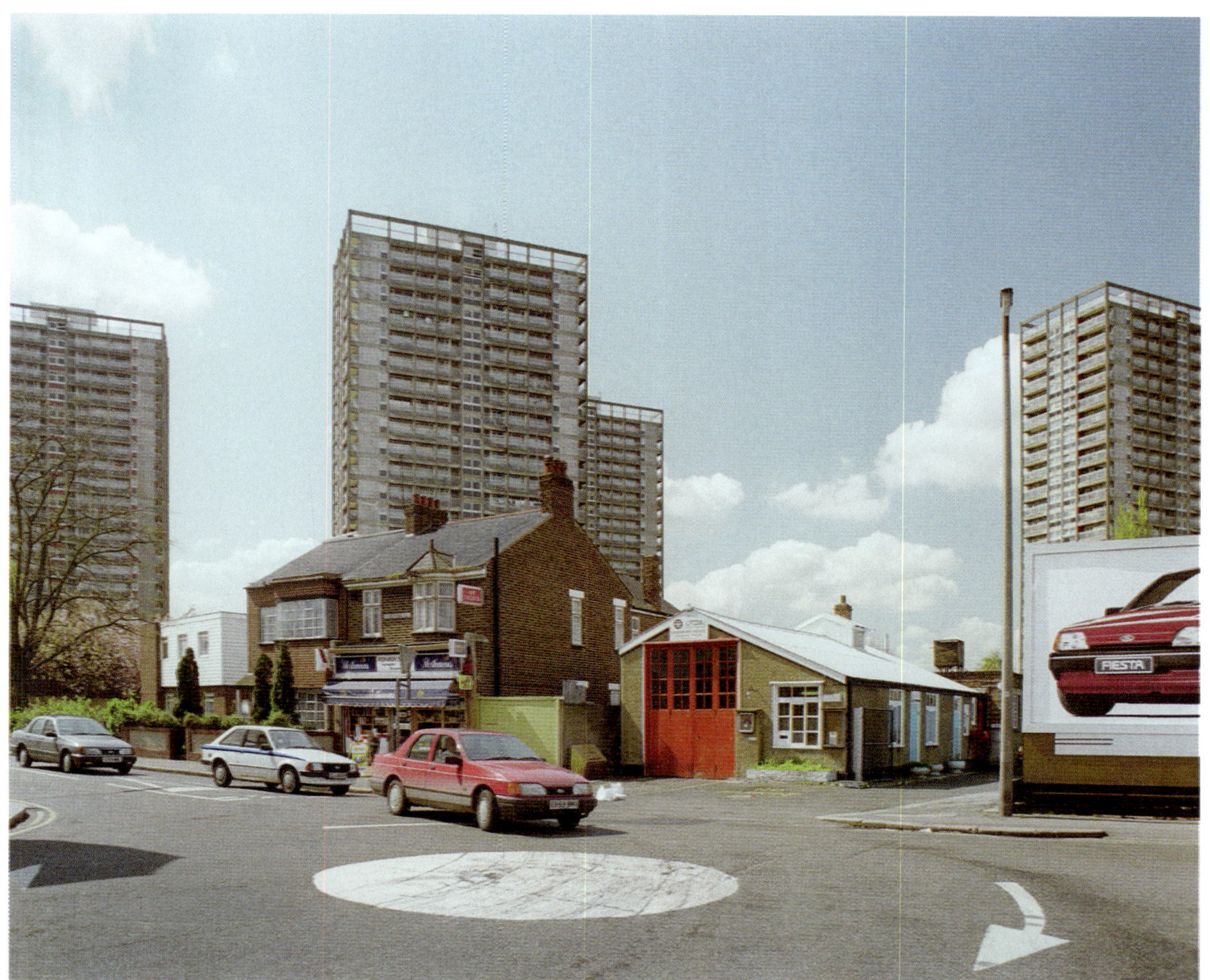

Leyton fire station, Church Road, 1989

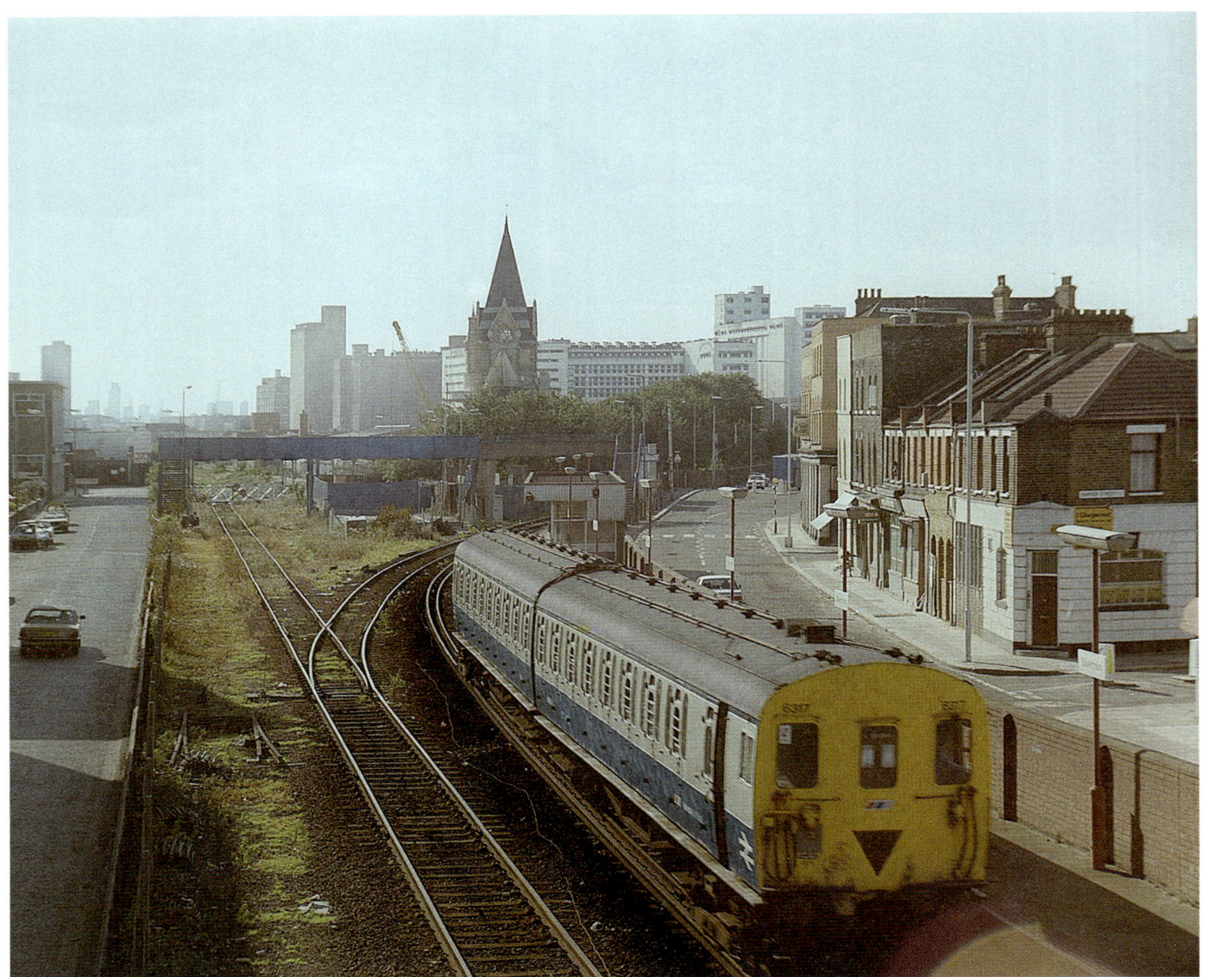

Silvertown station, 1987

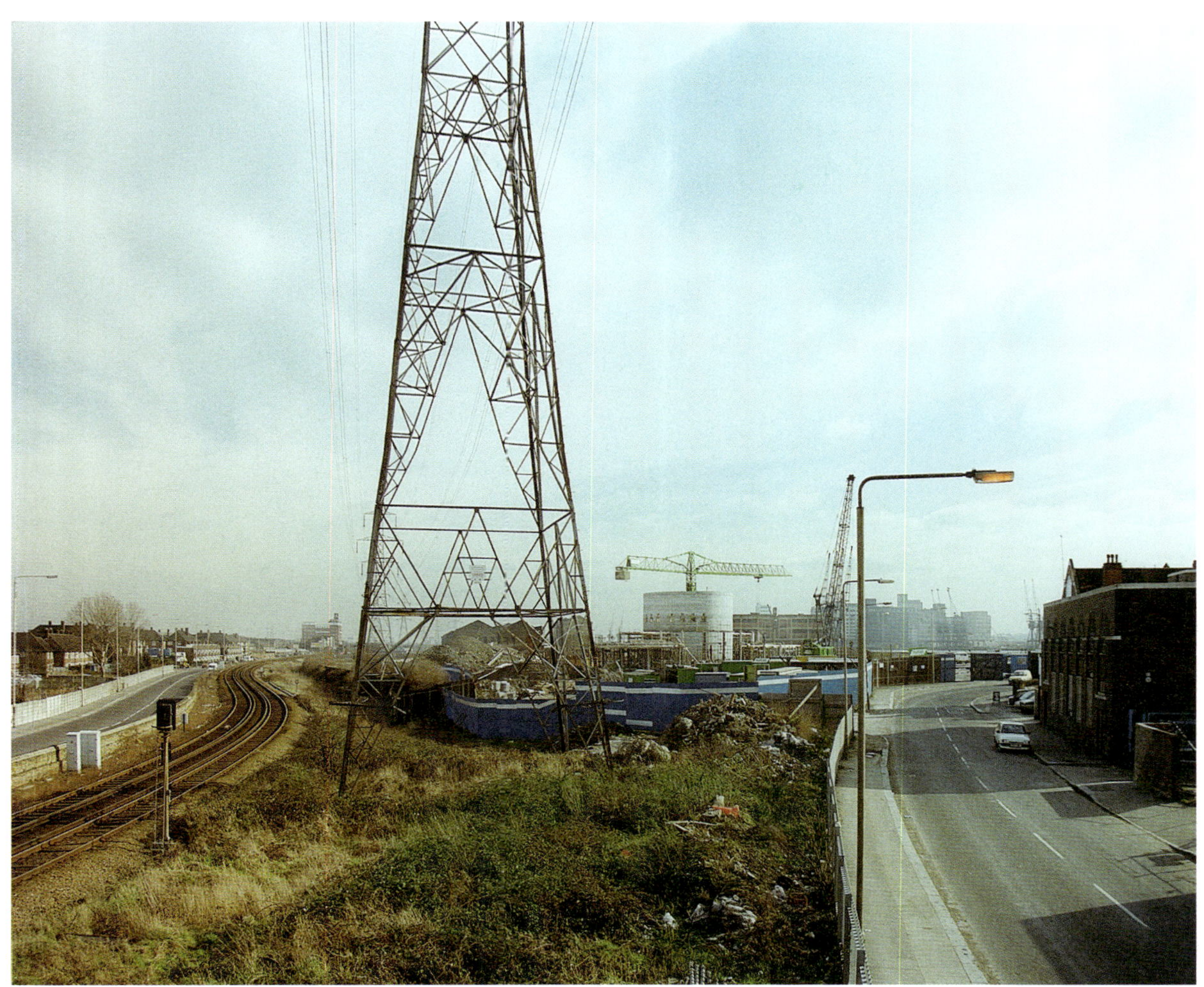

View of Tidal Basin from Silvertown Way, 1989

Silvertown tramway, 1987

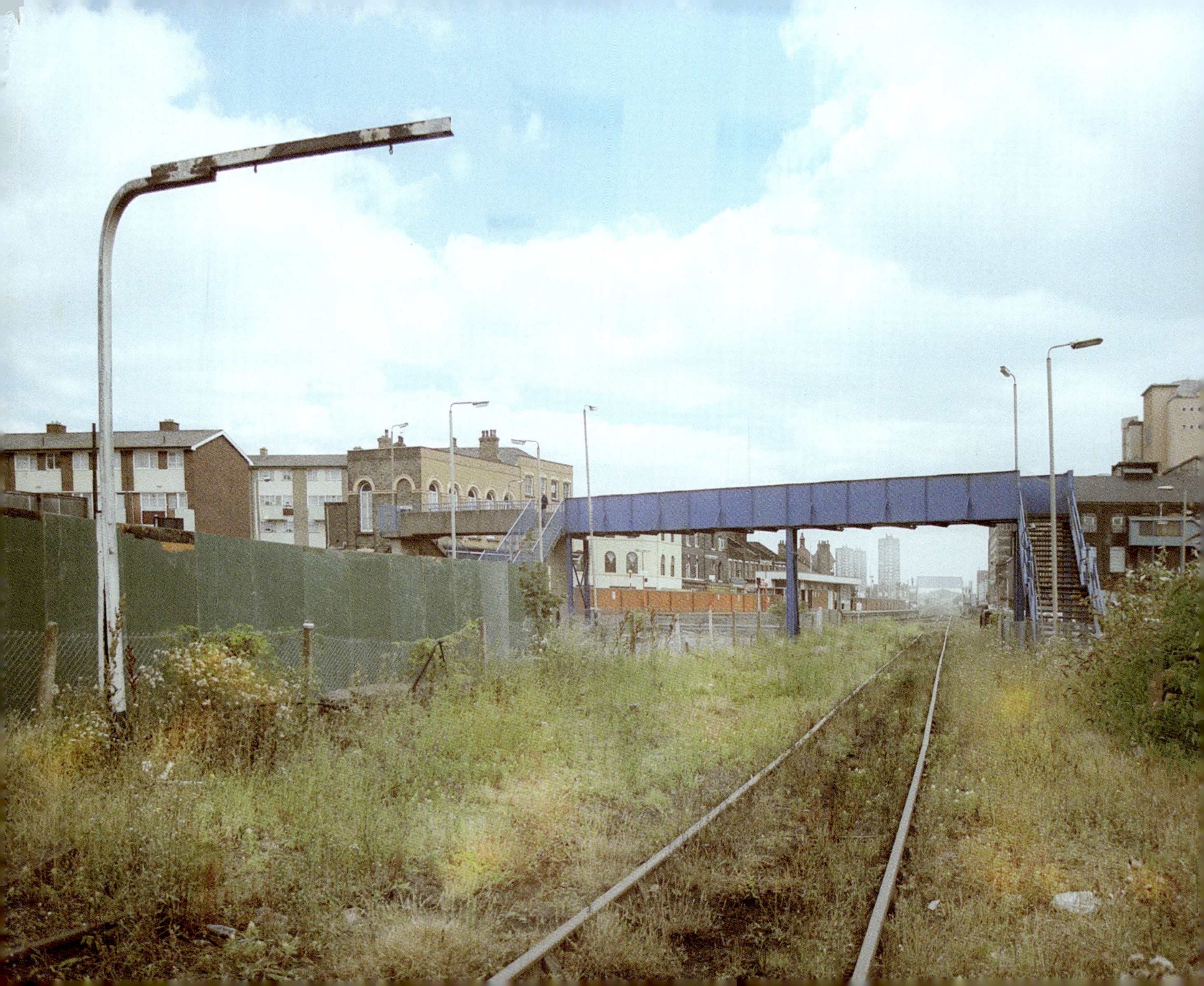

The East End in Colour 1980–1990

First edition, third printing, 2021

For Nikola, Natasha and Anton

Copyright © Hoxton Mini Press 2019. All rights reserved.
All photographs © Tim Brown, edited by Chris Dorley-Brown
Design and sequence by Friederike Huber, Chris Dorley-Brown and Hoxton Mini Press

Interview with Tim Brown conducted on 11 December 2018 in London
by Chris Dorley-Brown. Thanks to Chris for his careful work in digitising these
colour negatives and bringing them to our attention.

ISBN 978-1-910566-53-4

First published in the United Kingdom in 2019 by Hoxton Mini Press.
A CIP catalogue record for this book is available from the British Library.
No part of this publication may be reproduced, stored in a retrieval system, or transmitted
in any form or by any means, electronic, mechanical, photocopying, recording or otherwise,
without the prior written permission of the copyright owner.

Repro by Touch Digital. Production, design and editorial support from
Anna De Pascale, Daniele Roa and Faith McAllister at Hoxton Mini Press.

Printed and bound by OZGraf, Poland

To order books, collector's editions and signed prints please go to:
www.hoxtonminipress.com